THE SOCIETY OF MAN

THE
SOCIETY OF MAN

By

LOUIS J. HALLE

HARPER & ROW, PUBLISHERS
New York and Evanston

JX
1308
.H34
1965

51155

Printed in Great Britain
for Harper & Row, Publishers, Incorporated

'Man is the only animal that laughs and weeps; for he is the only animal that is struck with the difference between what things are, and what they ought to be.'

'Man is a make-believe animal—he is never so truly himself as when he is acting a part.'

Henry Hazlitt

CONTENTS

7

CONTENTS

PART THREE

Which examines the evolutionary process by which man creates himself, his dual world being driven forward by reciprocal action between the conceptual and the existential; and which suggests the consequent direction that the society of man is taking.

CONTENTS

9

PREFACE

Any general description of international relations is bound to rest on a philosophical foundation, whether tacit or explicit. An account of international relations may assume, for example, that states have a reality equivalent to that of individual persons. In such an account one may read how France moved to thwart Germany's purpose, or how the Latin American states brought the United States to accept them as its equals. Another account, assuming that modern governments represent 'peoples' and that 'peoples' are distinct entities, may report that 'the peoples' of the world agreed upon the Charter of United Nations at San Francisco in 1945, or that 'the German people' had been responsible for the outbreak of the two World Wars. Such assumptions belong to one philosophy or another.

Everyone who discourses on international relations, then, does so on the basis of a philosophy, even though he may remain unaware of the fact. Most writers base what they have to say on philosophical premises of such general acceptance, whether true or not, that they and their readers alike can take them for granted. Between such writers and their readers is the bond of common sense.

My difficulty arises out of the fact that, over the years, I became dissatisfied with this common sense. Much of what we tacitly assume came to seem to me doubtful or untrue. Over the years, then, I turned my attention to the philosophical foundations of our common thought. This brought me, at last, to the formulation of the philosophical system that I set forth in *Men & Nations*.

Since the present volume represents that philosophical

system, the reader may well ask whether *Men & Nations* has to be read first.

Fortunately it does not. All the relevant aspects of the philosophy set forth in the earlier book are brought out here wherever they are relevant. There should be no difficulty for the reader. The philosophy is a simple dualism, based on the elementary distinction between the tangible world and the conceptual world. The consistent and conscious application of this distinction to the phenomena of international relations seems to me essential for their understanding. But an understanding of what underlies the distinction is not.

The distinction, in itself, is banal: everyone who thinks about these things accepts it in principle, even if not applying it in such a pervasive and deliberate way as I have here. What is not altogether banal is the philosophy that explains it, but since I have dealt with that in the earlier book I need not deal with it again here. I could not have written the chapters that follow without first writing *Men & Nations*, without first building the platform. The reader, however, will find that to stand on that platform he does not need to concern himself with the scaffolding underneath.

Let nothing I say, however, discourage any reader who has a mind for whatever is behind what is behind international relations from reading the earlier book. The present book, in fact, would serve as a helpful introduction to it and ought, perhaps, to be read first in any case.

* * *

The chapters that follow illustrate the dualism of the world by reference to problems that confront the teacher of international relations, by reference to the history of Marxism, by reference to peculiarities of nationalism, and by reference to the evolution of mankind. Their intention is twofold: to illustrate the dualism by examples and to illuminate the examples by the dualism. They represent applied philosophy. In their conclusion they represent philosophy applied to the challenge of prophecy, concerning itself with the direction in which the society of man is moving.

They began as lectures that I gave over the academic year 1962–3 at the Graduate Institute of International Studies in Geneva. My intention was merely to transcribe my lecture-notes, but there is a demon inside me who will never let me do anything that easy. Once at work, I found myself reorganizing and reformulating everything. In the process, my own thoughts developed and presented their demands. It is always easier to begin a book casually than to go on that way. Few of us would ever set out to climb any mountain if we allowed ourselves to recognize how much farther away its summit was than, in the optimistic dawn-light, it appeared to be. Halfway up, one may be sorry one ever started. When at last one stands on the summit, however, there is pure exaltation. Then one knows, as those below never do, that mountain-climbing is what life is for.

* * *

I acknowledge here my special indebtedness to Dr. Istvàn Agoston, who hunted down citations for me in the libraries of Brussels, Berne, and Geneva, and who saved me from error by intelligent investigation. Both Professor Robert C. Tucker of Princeton University and Dr. Miklós Molnár of the Graduate Institute were kind enough to read Part Two in draft, and the critical comments of each were most helpful in the final revision. I am grateful, as well, to various other persons who gave me an occasional hand along the way. I alone am responsible for whatever mistakes remain.

Geneva, 1965   L. J. H.

PART ONE

Which shows how teaching and practice represent, respectively, the two worlds that all of us inhabit simultaneously: the orderly conceptual world and the chaotic existential world.

Chapter 1

PRACTICE *vs.* TEACHING

ANYONE who has experienced international relations in a foreign office, on the one hand, and as taught in the universities, on the other, knows that they are not the same thing. The difference, which is fundamental, may be taken as the point of departure for the construction of a whole philosophy.

The immediate presumption, especially in an empirical society like our own, is that the difference ought not to exist. International relations as practiced in foreign offices is the real thing, and the real thing is what ought to be taught.

This view became dominant in the United States at the end of the Second World War. There was a revulsion against the utopianism that had characterized the teaching of international relations in the period between the two wars. In that period professors of international relations had commonly been preachers and prophets, preaching international law, prophesying the collapse of civilization unless international law and international organization were made to prevail. They drew attention to the world as it should be, and in doing so they often drew attention away from the world as it was. Like educators teaching young people the ideal beauty of the marriage relationship while relegating prostitution to the realm of unmentionables, they commonly felt it their mission to turn the new generation away from the facts of power-politics, lest the knowledge of those facts bring the acceptance that men tend to accord to all established realities.

It is true that the teaching of diplomatic history inevitably exemplified the power-politics practiced in the foreign offices, but then they were generally represented as the practice of narrow or cynical men. This idealistic bias deepened whatever gulf already existed between the men in the universities and those in the foreign offices. Accustomed as they were to public misunderstanding, the foreign-office men were able to accept their bad repute among the intellectuals with indifference or with the disdain they have always felt for their unworldly critics.

This situation changed in the United States after World War II with the revolutionary change in our international position. The change occurred simultaneously on both sides of the gulf, in the universities and in the Department of State. In the universities a rebellion against utopianism was stimulated by the published observations of a foreign-office man, George Kennan, nourished by the continuous commentary of Walter Lippmann, and led by the outraged realism of Hans Morgenthau. The rising school of realists accepted power-politics as an inescapable fact of life, like any manifestation of original sin.

At the same time, the men in the State Department were in trouble deeper than any they had ever known. They were without a foreign policy to guide them. The traditional policy of non-involvement in the power-politics of other continents lay in ruins. The policy of getting along with Moscow would no longer work, and the effort to make it work threatened disaster. China was turning hostile. In Latin America, the bloom was off the Good Neighbor Policy. The State Department's wartime planning for the post-war world had produced little more than a loss of self-confidence. The military Fortinbras were being brought into the Department and into the highest councils of the government to make good the default of the civilian Hamlets. One heard a great deal of the need for long-range thinking and long-range planning in those days, and the State Department men tried to organize themselves for it. But they had no philosophy, no theory, no body of applicable principles on which to act. Their efforts at planning generally bogged down in topical questions, such as what to do with the Italian cable under the Atlantic, or what price to pay for tin. Under the circumstances, it was natural that they should look to the universities, where international affairs were being studied, for help.

There was a period after the War when various departments of the government tried to marry themselves to the universities. This worked in the case of the Pentagon and the faculties of science and technology, a wartime precedent having already been established at Oak Ridge and Los Alamos. In the case of the State Department it did not work. Professors of diplomatic history, professors of Latin American history, professors of economics and of sociology were brought to Washington for meetings at which the men in the State Department tried to explain their troubles. But the gulf could not be bridged. The professors tended to confine themselves to the general nature of the problems that the officials hopefully set before them, often speaking about the need to maintain the traditional idealism of our international conduct. When confronted by the direct question, 'What shall we *do*?' they fell silent. They could answer every question up to that last, but that last was the one question for which the men in the State Department had to have an answer.

The experiment, abandoned at last, left the State Department men in a mood of disenchantment tinged with bitterness, such as often follows a frustrated courtship or a broken engagement. They felt that the professors in their academic isolation had lost touch with reality. One reaction to this was the development, in influential quarters, of the view that the departments teaching international relations in the universities should be given a necessary transfusion of realism by having men whose experience was that of practitioners added to their faculties. The universities, themselves, were not hostile to this view.

As one of the practitioners who subsequently moved from the State Department into the academic world, I can now testify, after almost a decade of academic experience, that the balance of benefit flowed the other way. I had more to learn than to teach.

*   *   *

When the practitioner crosses over into the academic world he has suddenly to face the question of just what he will teach. What his sponsors and employers expect of him is that he will teach the reality of international relations, *i.e.*, those matters with which he had had to deal as a practitioner. He quickly finds out, however, that there is a distinction between what is teachable and what is not, and that those matters belong to the category of what is not teachable.

I shall, in the first instance, try to show the nature of the distinction by two examples. While I was still in the government, several of my colleagues and I attended a lecture in which a high official of the State Department undertook to explain how policy was made inside it. Here was the practitioner in the role of teacher. In his hand was a pointer, and on the wall behind him was an organization-chart of the Department, showing the usual pyramid: the Office of the Secretary of State at the top, the various divisions and subdivisions ramifying downward, becoming more specialized, until at the bottom one ended with 'country desks' and offices responsible for the narrowest functional specialties. The procedures of the Department, we were told, all fell into one or the other of two categories: policy-making and policy-implementation. Policy-making was centralized, policy-implementation decentralized. Policy was made at the top, by the Secretary and his advisers, and then communicated downward through the Department. Implementation was initiated at the lowest level and carried upward for clearance. (I don't know whether implementation going up ever col-

lided with policy coming down.) The lecture was so per-
suasive that only afterwards, when its spell had begun to
wear off, did it come to our minds that, in point of fact, the
Department did not function that way at all. The practitioner turned teacher had also turned utopian for the occasion. What he had taught us was not the reality but an
ideal model.

What, then, was the reality?

Again, I can only exemplify in terms of personal experience, supplemented by personal inquiry. In 1948 the government had for some years been conducting programs of
technical assistance in Latin America, and only there. It
seemed reasonable that this novel way of conducting international relations might have its uses elsewhere in the world
as well, and I recall one occasion especially, a late evening
at the end of the day's work, when the Deputy Director of
American Republic Affairs and I talked casually about this
possibility.

Then, sometime in November, a routine message from
the President's speech-writing assistant in the White House
requested the Department to send over, in due course, any
proposals it had for the contents of the Inaugural Address
that the President was to deliver in January. Following
established procedure in these matters, the Director of the
Office of Public Affairs called a meeting of the interested
divisions, to which my friend the Deputy Director went in
representation of American Republic Affairs. A Mr. Ben
Hardy, pad on knee, took down the various proposals put
forward at the meeting as they were accepted. The first
proposal advanced and accepted was a statement of support
for the United Nations; second was an assurance that the
European Recovery Program would be continued; third,
the announcement of an intention to organize a common
defense among the free nations of the Atlantic area.

Any more?

There was a pause while everyone searched his mind. The Deputy Director, recalling our evening conversation, ended the pause by asking: how about technical assistance for undeveloped countries (the word 'underdeveloped' had not yet been coined), like what we're doing in Latin America?

That's a good idea, said the Director of Public Affairs, put it down, Ben. So 'Point Four' was set down without further discussion, and there the meeting adjourned.

When the four points proposed for inclusion in the President's address went up through the Department's clearance-machinery, the fourth was discarded. Here I do not have the details, but I have no difficulty in surmising. Any responsible officer was bound to ask what thought and analysis had entered into the proposal of a program for giving technical assistance to countries all over the world. What countries specifically? What kinds of technical assistance, specifically? On what scale? How much would it cost? Until at least rough answers to these questions were available, until at least the feasibility of such a program had been determined, it would be irresponsible to have the President announce it. So the first three points, without the fourth, were sent on to the White House.

A few days later, the Director of Public Affairs received a 'phone-call from the presidential assistant, who complained that, while the three points were OK in themselves, they were mere 'boiler-plate' (government slang for the cant statements that are always thrown into speeches). I think, he said, the President would like to have something in this speech that's just a bit original.

At this juncture, without proper time for reflection, the Director of Public Affairs found himself standing on the shore of his own Rubicon. He took a deep breath, and crossed over.

There had been a fourth point, he said, but it had been thrown out.

What was it?

The Director told what it was.

That's great, said the voice from the White House, and 'Point Four' went back in again.

If anyone gave the matter a further thought, from that moment until the delivery of the Address on January 20, I find no indication of it. 'Point Four' was a public-relations gimmick, thrown in by a professional speech-writer to give the speech more life.

When the newspapers dramatized it in their principal headlines on the morning of January 21, the White House and the State Department were taken completely by surprise. No one—not the President, not the Secretary of State, not the presidential assistant or the Director of Public Affairs—knew any more about 'Point Four' than what they could read for themselves in the meager and rather rhetorical language of the speech. No one could answer the pressing questions of the newspaper-reporters, of the Congressmen concerned with appropriations, of the foreign diplomats. It was only now, after the Inaugural Address had been delivered and the 'bold new program' acclaimed all over the world, that machinery was set up in the government to look into the possibilities of such a program and make plans. The inauguration of an actual program was not to come until twenty-one months later—twenty-one months of hard-packed confusion in which the careers of good men were broken and ulcers proliferated.

These two examples—the lecture on policy-making in the Department, the actual making of the 'Point Four' policy—exemplify the contrast between teaching and practice. What is taught is an ordered and formal scheme; what happens in practice is unordered, a succession of accidents.

The question is whether what we professors ought to teach is the formal scheme or, rather, the succession of accidents. The formal scheme is readily teachable. There are, however,

intrinsic difficulties in teaching what is formless and accidental. Accidents lack regularity, they are different accidents
on every occasion. The formal scheme is a prediction, a prediction of what will happen tomorrow and the next day
whenever a policy-question arises. The succession of accidents, always unique in its occurrence, is unpredictable. The
succession of accidents by which the 'Point Four' policy
came to be made was without precedent and would not be
repeated in the production of other policies, each of which
would be the consequence of an equally unique succession
of accidents. The particular succession of accidents that
results in the birth of any particular policy represents chaos
rather than order. While we may dip into chaos for samples
to describe, each sample is unique. Chaos itself, chaos as
a whole, cannot be described, and therefore it cannot be
taught.

In principle, following the precept to teach the reality
experienced by the practitioners, one might recount the
sequel of accidental events that culminated in each policy
worthy of academic concern—doing, let us say, for the Good
Neighbor Policy, for the Truman Doctrine, for the Marshall Plan, and so forth, what I have done partially, as an
example, for 'Point Four.'

I leave aside, for the moment, the question of the purpose
to be served by feeding students on chaos, by asking them to
learn endless series of accidental events, of events without
meaning in which it is doubtful that any regularities could be
found. (If any were found, then the realm of accident would
be transcended *ipso facto*.) Whatever answer we made, the
fact would remain that the material for such teaching does
not exist.

In consequence of a unique personal opportunity (such as
never comes to most teachers) I have been able to reconstruct,
roughly, the circumstances in which 'Point Four' was born.
The material on which I have based my reconstruction would

not ordinarily be accepted as reliable in scholarly circles: it consists of my own memory of events and my memory of what others later told me they remembered. In this case I don't doubt its essential truth because the circumstances are few and simple, the Deputy Director of American Republic Affairs and the Director of Public Affairs were speaking to me informally as a colleague, in the intimacy of the official family, shortly after the events in question, and I was myself close to those events from the beginning to the end. (Moreover, research would tend to corroborate it by showing, if only negatively, that no plans, not even any preliminary sketches, had been made for 'Point Four' prior to its announcement.) I could offer such a reconstruction, however, for nothing else in my years of governmental experience, so that I would have to stop my teaching when, after two or three lectures, I had exhausted my practitioner's experience of 'Point Four.' This kind of information is in the highest degree evanescent, so that it is altogether exceptional to have managed to preserve just one sample of it, such as the one I have presented here. Even so, the accepted version of how 'Point Four' was born—the version that will enter the history books and be taught—is quite different. As we shall see further on in this chapter, it is tidier and more creditable to our dignity as creatures moved by reason and intelligent purpose.

The process of bringing order out of chaos begins to operate on events as soon as they have taken place. And only the order that ensues, not the original chaos, lends itself to teaching.

We are faced with all sorts of limits. What the professor of history teaches is not and cannot be history at the making of which he was present. What the professor of comparative government teaches is not and cannot be governmental processes in which he has been personally involved. The professor can see his subject only from afar, in a perspective from which the welter of accidental circumstances, experienced only at point-blank range, has disappeared.

Suppose I have to lecture on the government of the Dominican Republic, in which I have never served. I depend on the standard sources of information available to any scholarly inquirer. These, for reasons which we know, set forth the formal situation, what represents order rather than chaos. They set forth, primarily, the normative ideal that can never be fully realized in practice. What I shall find myself teaching specifically is the Dominican Constitution, which is modeled on that of the United States. I shall teach the separation of powers, legislative, executive, and judicial, enumerating the constitutional limits imposed on each. I shall do as the lecturer on policy-making in the State Department did. I shall teach what is teachable, which is to say that I shall teach the ideal model. In this exceptional case, I may supplement and qualify that teaching with an account of how the spirit and letter of the Dominican Constitution were violated during the presidency of Generalissimo Trujillo, since what is exceptional about this case is the degree to which the violations became notorious and therefore available as information. (Note that, in the case of the State Department's formal procedures for policy-making, the violations in the making of the 'Point Four' policy did not become available as information.)

Again, if I teach the United Nations my primary teaching will be of the Charter, article by article—this, rather than what goes on privately in the corridors of the United Nations Building and does not come to my ears.

With my colleagues, I used to wonder that international law loomed so large in the teaching of international relations, when a year might go by in the Office of the Secretary of State without any appreciable question of international law arising. Today I no longer wonder.

Perhaps the only advantage that the teacher gains from

practical experience—but it is an immense and fundamental advantage—is in his poignant awareness of the fact that what he teaches is not the whole truth, that it is a sort of mythical truth, that there is an enormous and chaotic existential world outside it which his teaching hardly touches—the world of the practitioner.

*   *   *

Officers of the Department of State who deal with foreign diplomats or with the representatives of other governmental departments make memoranda of all conversations that it would be well to have on record. As soon as possible after a foreign diplomat has 'phoned an officer or dropped in on him to discuss some item of official business, the officer calls in a stenographer and dictates a 'Memorandum of Conversation.' In it he reports what the other party said, what he said in reply, and so forth.

A veteran of the State Department once remarked that in the course of his career he had read thousands of Memoranda of Conversation, yet never one in which the officer who drafted it had reported any delay on his part in finding just the right thing to say, no matter how unexpected or upsetting the words of the other party.

The observation was more than witty, it was true. Few of us have minds so quick, so penetrating, and so efficient that we immediately make the right response to an interlocutor's every challenge. On the contrary, we hem and haw, we say the wrong thing and try to recover the situation too late, or what we should have said comes into our minds only afterwards. Nevertheless, the process of tidying up the record, of tidying up history itself, begins as early as this. It begins within seconds of the event.

At the beginning of our participation in the Second World War the Department was engaged in a long and complex diplomatic campaign to have the telecommunications circuits between the Axis and the two neutral countries in Latin America, Argentina and Chile, discontinued. Information gained by espionage and delivered through these circuits was enabling Hitler's submarines to intercept and sink allied shipping in the Atlantic. In those days, even on matters of great importance, junior officers were encouraged to initiate action on their own, subject to the clearance of their superiors. As the most junior officer involved in this campaign, the one who sat silent at the meetings of the big chiefs and then drafted the action that had been decided on, I availed myself freely of the initiative that was mine. I was young, I was new to the government, the great matters of life and death were in hand, and I threw myself into the work with the elation of being engaged in a high and adventurous enterprise. It was like a novel, and it finished like a novel with a happy ending. The circuits were broken, ships and men were saved; from that point we marched on triumphantly to finish the War. Often, in my daydreams, I thought about the achievement, how ingenious we had been and how well we had done. I went over the facts in my mind. If a historian had come to me then and asked how we had succeeded in getting the circuits broken, I could have told him that he had come to the one man in all the world who knew the story best; for, while the men at the top had seen what went on at the top, I was the only one who had seen the whole thing from top to bottom. I was the man to tell him, and I would have done so with assurance.

It was less than a year after these events that I had occasion to visit the Department's archives in search of a document difficult to identify. In the course of my search I came across the whole file of documents on the breaking of the circuits: memoranda and telegrams, instructions to our ambassadors, dispatches from them. When I sat down and began to go through them, as I immediately did, what had really happened came back to me, and it was quite different from what had developed in my memory with the lapse of time. It was less simple and less tidy; it was more confused; it was closer to chaos.

Experience has shown me that the faults of memory illustrated by this event are not peculiar to me.

At President Truman's press-conference, six days after the Inaugural Address in which he electrified the world with his announcement of the 'Point Four' program, he was asked: 'Mr. President, can you give us any background on the origin of Point Four?'

The origin of Point Four [he replied] has been in my mind, and in the minds of the government, for the past two or three years, ever since the Marshall Plan was inaugurated. It originated with the Greece and Turkey propositions. Been studying it ever since. I spend most of my time going over to that globe back there, trying to figure out ways to make peace in the world.

The human mind cannot deal with chaos; it can get no grip on it. By translating chaos it preserves its sanity, which depends on order. Indeed, its basic function is to bring order out of chaos. The scholar is not different from the artist in this, the historian or the political scientist is not different from the novelist. All are equally engaged in the necessary task of ordering chaos.

I have emphasized the role of accident in what actually happens. Its role, however, is dominant only in the close-up view. In the close-up view, if the Deputy Director of American Republic Affairs and I had not speculated idly together as we did after the day's work, if the Deputy Director had not gone to a certain meeting, if he had not happened to recall our conversation while at that meeting, if the Director of Public Affairs had been so discreet as not to mention to the President's assistant what had been dropped from the Department's proposals—then there would have been no 'Point Four.'

I cannot believe, however, that this close-up view is right.

As someone afterwards said, 'Point Four' was 'in the air' at the time, as Darwin's theory of evolution had been 'in the air' when he published his *Origin of Species*. If Darwin had never been born, Alfred Russel Wallace would have published an equivalent work, and if not he then someone else. If the series of accidents that produced 'Point Four' had not occurred, another series of accidents would have produced it in another way, under another name. I put myself, here, on the side of order, and I shall undertake in later chapters to justify my doing so.

The chaotic actuality that I described in reporting the genesis of 'Point Four' has no ultimate importance in itself. It is just as well for it to be lost from the record. The historian who reports faithfully will say that, in the late 1940's, technical assistance for underdeveloped countries was 'in the air,' that it represented the logic of the world situation, and he will not concern himself overmuch with whether President Truman or someone else invented it out of the resources of his own mind. It will be proper for him to regard all these accidentals of the close-up view with scepticism, and to regard them as not properly belonging to history although they may occasionally serve, where they can be determined with confidence, to embellish it. The history of the world would not really have been different if Cleopatra's nose had been shorter.

The practitioner lives the closest to chaos. He is beset by accidents at every turn: someone taken sick, a 'plane grounded by the weather, a friendly government upset by an unexpected scandal, a ship sunk or a statesman kidnapped or a message undelivered. These accidents seem to him decisive at the time, and so they become his entire preoccupation. His job, in effect, becomes the management of chaos by rapid improvisation. This is why the situation always looks so desperate at the seat of government, in times that history will call successful no less than in times of failure.

The scholar should, as such, keep out of all this. He does not belong to it, and as a scholar he cannot function in terms of it. He should not, therefore, think himself capable of saying how the practical problems of the daily chaos should be solved, of telling the practitioner what to do. He should resist the temptation of making a government's topical decisions vicariously, or announcing how it should make them, thanking his stars that, since those decisions can be finally made only at the seat of responsibility, like the decisions that only a commander on the battlefield can make, he is not called upon to bear the perplexity and the risk of having to make them himself.

'It is the gift of civilized man,' Walter Lippmann once wrote, '. . . that he can at times see through the transient and the complicated to the simple and the certain, and that he can live by that vision, and with it master or endure his lot.' The exercise of this gift is the scholar's real business. It is his real business (again in Lippmann's words) to see 'the necessary amidst confusion and insignificance, and by the light which it furnishes to see more clearly how to act with purpose.'[1] The scholar's business is direction. He is like the navigator of a ship, who does not himself take the wheel but makes the calculations on the basis of which the actions of the man at the wheel can be addressed, as opportunity serves, to a purpose beyond the immediate moment. If the sea is chaotic, the man at the wheel will have to be pre-occupied with every looming wave that threatens the ship, and will have to act quickly either to evade or meet it, even though this means acting with apparent inconsistency, turning first in one direction, then in another. But these waves are not the navigator's business, and he will only confuse himself and the helmsman if he tries to make them his business. His business is to see beyond 'the transient and

[1] *The Essential Lippmann*, Rossiter & Lare (editors), New York, 1963, pp. 76–7.

the complicated,' and to make known what he sees, so that the ship can in the long run realize a purpose beyond that of survival in the present, so that it can have direction.

*   *   *

The question is what should be taught when we teach international relations. With my colleagues in government I once assumed that what should be taught was the reality as we knew it in our close-up view. We have seen, however, that this is hardly possible. There is no way of lifting the experience out of the foreign offices in its raw, unprocessed state, as it is at the instant of being experienced, and displaying it to students in classrooms. It is too beset by confusion and insignificance. It is too perishable, for we have seen how the mind begins to translate it within seconds of its occurrence. The practitioner's experience is merely the chaos out of which we have to make some order, whether a true or a false order, before we can present it to our students.

The reader will note the importance of the question implicitly raised in the phrase, 'whether a true or a false order.' This question is at the heart of all human culture; it is the point of departure for all science and all art. In its largest aspect it is the central question of the universe. We shall have to deal with it at some stage in the present discussion. For the moment I merely observe that, while the international relations that are taught must be different from the international relations experienced by the practitioner, the one ought not to be without some relevance to the other.

Chapter 2

THE GAP BETWEEN TWO WORLDS

In 1952, while both sides in the Korean War were engaged in the armistice negotiations at Panmunjon, the Communist governments of North Korea and of China publicly accused the United Nations forces under American leadership of having resorted to germ-warfare in North Korea and Manchuria. American 'planes were said to have dropped bacteria-bearing insects behind the North Korean lines in an effort to spread cholera, typhus, and bubonic plague. Although the International Red Cross was not allowed to send neutral experts to the Communist territory to investigate, the circumstantial nature of the accusations made them seem plausible. The Communists even succeeded in producing, for the news-cameras, American prisoners-of-war who testified that they were United States Air Force men who had flown germ-spreading missions in which they had dropped the containers of germs. I was in a position to feel sure that the government in Washington had not authorized the use of bacteriological agents by the forces in Korea, but as the accusations were repeated and new circumstantial details reported I began to wonder whether a local commander might not have resorted to these agents on his own. I was soon satisfied that this was not the case. Lack of adequate public-health facilities had led to the outbreak of epidemics in North Korea and Manchuria, and the governmental authorities, it appears, invented the germ-warfare charges to explain them.

From our point of view, and also in a strictly objective sense, these governmental authorities were lying. From their own point of view, however, there was a sense in which they were not lying. Let me take the example of a photograph

c

33

51155

that they gave to the press, showing a battered canister in a plowed field. The caption explained that this canister, containing infected insects, had been dropped from an American 'plane. In a literal sense this was false: the canister, we may be sure, had been provided and placed where it was by the Communists themselves, to be photographed as evidence in support of the accusations they were making.

Brought up as we are to a regard for the literal truth, we are shocked by the dishonesty of this device. From the point of view of the Communists, however, it may not have been essentially dishonest. Their mental processes are based on *a priori* knowledge of what to them constitutes unquestionable truth. This *a priori* knowledge tells them that the 'ruling classes' in 'capitalist, imperialist' countries necessarily behave in certain reprehensible ways, and that it is the mission of all good Communists to expose these ways to the world. It is in the nature of these 'ruling classes' to be without scruple in their warfare against 'the people.' The resort to germ-warfare is therefore representative of their true behavior. It represents an *a priori* truth, and so is 'true' in an essential sense, in the only sense that counts. If in a particular contingency the capitalists happen not to have employed the particular device of germ-warfare, this is an accidental truth only. Consequently, in the accidental absence of actual pieces of material evidence to photograph, the artful provision of such evidence is justifiable as a way of illustrating the truth that counts.

Just as the lecturer on the subject of how policy is made in the State Department had an ideal model in mind, so the Communists who planted the evidence for germ-warfare had an ideal model in mind: the model of a world divided between 'the people,' who are good, and 'the enemies of the people,' who are wicked. In planting the evidence for the wickedness of the latter they were simply bringing the one true order out of chaos, making it manifest to mankind.

By contrast with a Communist society, in which doctrinal unity is imposed, our society (at least in its ideal model) enjoys the freedom that permits diversity. We are free to disagree over the alternative conceptual orders, the alternative models, that compete for our allegiance. This does not mean, however, that we are less governed than the Communists by ideal models. An officer of the State Department, in his conversation with a foreign diplomat, is trying to live up to an ideal model for his behavior that exists as a concept in his mind. According to that model, he immediately finds just the right answer to make to the foreign diplomat at every turn of the conversation. On any particular occasion, it is true, the element of accident (representing the chaos out of which we are all trying to struggle) will enter in. He may have an unaccountable mental lapse that causes him for a moment to miss the real significance of what his interlocutor is saying; or there may be a 'slip of the tongue' in his own response. In memory, however, these accidental factors disappear, the ideal model reasserts itself, order is restored. His Memorandum of Conversation represents the beginning of the process by which chaos is translated back into the order that existed *a priori*. Essential truth is preserved.

There is a difference between the Communist behavior, exemplified by the faked evidence, and the behavior of the American official, but it is a limited difference and, I think, of degree only. The Communists, being brought up in a world that (at least in its ideal model) knows only one conceptual order, an order that stands unchallenged as the sole representation of truth, do not doubt that the whole truth is known to them. We, on the other hand, being brought up in a market-place where all sorts of rival and mutually exclusive conceptual orders compete for our acceptance, learn to doubt that any one order represents the finally attained truth. We acquire an agnostic bent of mind. We learn a certain scepticism of *a priori* doctrinal systems that makes us more empirical, that makes us more dependent on the facts of the existential world, that makes us more respectful of them, that makes us hesitate to disregard their literal truth for the sake of any such system. The action of faking the evidence would, I think, go against the conscience of most of us rather harder than against that of the Communists. This is of fundamental practical importance, but still a matter of degree. The official of the State Department would probably not allow himself, in his Memorandum of Conversation, to depart from the facts in any flagrant degree, but he allows himself to depart from them in ways regarded as innocent. On the other hand, I would not assert that the Communists were altogether without similar inhibitions that they have to overcome in order to undertake a flagrant departure from the facts.

*　　*　　*

Our problem is that we necessarily live, at one and the same time, in two disparate worlds: a chaotic existential world and a conceptual world of order. I say 'necessarily' because, if we attempted to do so, we would find it impossible to choose one and reject the other.

If I undertake to reject the existential world, as a solipsist does, saying it is all a dream, that it is all my own conception, that there is nothing outside my own mind, I shall simply find myself in the position of the faith-healer of Deal

> Who said, Although pain is not real,
> If I sit on a pin,
> And it punctures my skin,
> I dislike what I fancy I feel.

Although I deny that food is real, I shall fancy that I feel a craving for it and go after it all the same. Although I deny that the rain is real I shall seek shelter from it nevertheless.

Socrates, as Plato reports him, had leanings this way. Valuing the visions of his inner consciousness above all else, he regarded existential reality as a poor imitation. Oriental mystics have gone further, denying that the external material world exists at all. We, however, are a practical people who cannot solve our problems that way. Our disposition, rather, is to say that only the material world is real, that idealizations and other conceptual abstractions are merely nominal. In practice, however, we are as unable to reject the conceptual as the existential world. If it were possible for us to do so, to reject the conceptual world on the grounds that it was illusory, we would find that nothing was left except an existential chaos so complete as to be unimaginable. We could not reject the conceptual world without rejecting consciousness itself.

We understand nothing, our minds admit nothing, except in terms of some conceptual order. When we see a great light rise regularly on the eastern horizon, cross the sky, and disappear below the western horizon, we are drawn as conscious beings to find or devise an explanation, to evoke an order in the mind that will account for the phenomenon. We can no more avoid doing this than we can make our minds blank, excluding all images, notions, or thoughts. We are bound to provide ourselves at least with some tacit, unformulated explanation of the existential phenomenon, an explanation that represents the conceptual world. We may adopt, by way of explanation, the concept of a sun god; or we may adopt the concept of a fiery mass about which our planet revolves while spinning on its own axis. In any case, we can think of the existential phenomenon at all only in terms of a conceptual order that our minds impose on it. That conceptual order appeals to us as more valid or less according as it appears to correspond at all points with the existential phenomenon that it pretends to explain.

Since we have to live in both worlds at once, what concerns us in the first instance is the relation between them. In the example I just gave of the light that rises in the east, the conceptual world comes second, it follows the existential world by way of explanation. The same order of precedence was represented by the Memorandum of Conversation, which reported and, at the same time, translated prior existential happenings. In any process of creation, however, the conceptual comes first. The sculptor has a concept, an image in his mind, that he then renders in existential stone. It is certain that the conceptual order to which the existential facts were made to conform, in the Memorandum of Conversation, actually preceded those facts. It took the form of a concept of propriety that influenced the behavior of the State Department officer in his conversation with the foreign diplomat. The concept of propriety shaped his behavior with a success that could only be partial, and his impulse to correct his existential failures when he came to writing his report of the conversation represented the influence of the *a priori* concept, its persistence *ex post facto*. The planting of the putative germ-container by the Communists was an attempt, which has its pitiful and ludicrous aspects, to correct *ex post facto* the accidental failure of existential circumstances to conform to an *a priori* conceptual model.

In teaching, we may overlook the true relationship between conceptual models and existential realities. The organization-chart of the State Department, as explained by the lecturer, was an *a priori* conceptual model that the existential reality was expected to imitate; but he presented it as if it were the *ex post facto* description of a pre-existing reality in the existential world. I might likewise teach the Constitution of the Dominican Republic or the Charter of the United Nations as if it were a description of what had been observed, rather than an *a priori* model of what was intended.

At the beginning stages of human evolution, we may suppose, man's creative capacity had hardly begun, as yet, to manifest itself. He described his environment in conceptual terms, but it no more occurred to him that he might reform that environment (in accordance with conceptual models of his own invention) than it occurs to us that we might reverse the direction of the earth in its orbit. He accepted existential reality as given, and tried to understand it. Pure science precedes applied science.

In the course of our evolution, however, we men have shown an increasing aptitude to reshape our environment according to our conceptions. We have at last transformed the earth, so that anyone flying around it in an airplane can see to what an extent it has become, today, a man-made world. Man has become the creator. He has become the creator of himself, and he has become the creator of his environment. As the creator of his own behavior, he has now begun to direct his own biological evolution, thereby creating himself in a more fundamental sense.[1] With respect to the external environment, he has become the creator of objects of his own design: a statue, a building, an airplane, an artificial lake, a cultivated field, a highway. And in this process of creation, as in any process of creation, the conceptual world has priority over the existential. In the beginning is the word, and the word is made flesh.

*　　*　　*

What is the process of creation, the process by which a concept is translated into existential reality?

In its entirety it is a process more elaborate than I suggested in my example of the sculptor who shapes the stone in imitation of an image that he has in his mind. The statue itself is merely the expression of his concept, offered for the imitation of flesh-and-blood. It is an agency for communicating the sculptor's concept to those whose imitation is invited, and so it must be regarded as an intermediate stage in the process of creation. The women who cultivate figures like that of the Venus de Milo—or, more importantly, who cultivate in themselves the dignity and serenity

[1] See Chapter 10 for a discussion of this.

that it represents—constitute the final stage, the sculptor's true creation.

An architect has the concept of a house. He makes blueprints for the communication of that concept to men who will do the actual building. On the basis of these drawings the earth is measured off, bricks are laid, walls are erected, a roof is fastened to the walls—until at last the concept has been 'realized' in the finished existential house.

And is that the end?

'We shape our buildings,' said Winston Churchill, 'and then our buildings shape us.' He was referring, specifically, to the political processes imposed on government in England by the shape of the House of Commons; but our buildings shape us in innumerable and untold ways. The men who conduct government will be apt to manifest a greater nobility in its conduct if the government is housed in buildings that represent the cultural level of the Athenian acropolis than if it is housed in a slum. Finally, and in more general terms, the biological evolution of mankind represents a constant adaptation to the new environments that it creates, so that the men bred in cities will be biologically different from those bred in the aboriginal forests.[2]

As an architect has a concept of a building, so a political philosopher might have the concept of a state. Plato, for example, did have the concept of a state, of an ideal state, of what seemed to him the perfect state. He gave this concept expression in the form of a book, the *Republic*. The book was a nominal expression, an expression in language, a literary creation without any existential standing in itself—since it was independent of any one physical volume in which the language was conveyed by ink on paper. What Plato created was not, in its essence, an existential object but, rather, a concept set forth in language—a concept that might, for the most part, be quite untranslatable into existential

[2] See citation of Dobzhansky below, p. 155.

reality. Nobody, in fact, has ever attempted to set up Plato's ideal state.

Take, now, another and similar example. Sir Thomas More was a courtier and statesman at the court of King Henry VIII. Just as Shakespeare's Hamlet grew disgusted with the sordid existential reality of the Danish court, so Sir Thomas (an idealist like Hamlet) grew disgusted with the sordid existential reality of the English court. He took refuge from this existential reality by imagining another and a better land, a land for which he invented the name 'Utopia' (Greek for 'Nowhere'). Utopia is nowhere; it does not belong to the world of existential reality; it belongs exclusively to the conceptual world. As in the case of Plato's *Republic*, Sir Thomas More's creation was merely literary. Published in 1516, it became immensely popular, presumably offering its many readers a psychological escape from their sordid existential environment.

More's imaginary state had several radical features. One was religious freedom. Another was public education provided by the state for both sexes alike. These features were almost unthinkable (in modern parlance, they were utopian) in the England of Henry VIII. But today in England, in Sir Thomas More's country four and a half centuries later, religious freedom and state education for both sexes have become established. It is clear that the writing and publication of More's *Utopia* contributed to shaping the existential reality of England today, four and a half centuries later. It set forth a conceptual order that made its impress increasingly on men's minds, until they began translating it into existential reality.

After Plato's *Republic* and More's *Utopia*, let me take a third nominal document that belongs to essentially the same genre. This one opens with the words:

We the People of the United States, in Order to form a more perfect Union, establish Justice, insure domestic Tranquility, provide for the common defence, promote the General Welfare, and secure the Blessings of Liberty to ourselves and our Posterity, do ordain and establish this Constitution for the United States of America.

It then goes on to provide, among other things, that no law shall be made 'respecting an establishment of religion, or prohibiting the free exercise thereof'—and I mention this because it shows a connection with that other nominal creation, More's *Utopia*.

The Constitution of the United States, unlike More's *Utopia*, was deliberately drafted as the design for a state to be set up forthwith—a state that was, in fact, set up forthwith. Just as an architect has the concept of a house, and sets forth that concept in the form of blueprints, on the basis of which the finished house is built, so the authors of the Constitution had the concept of a state, and cast that concept in the form of this constitutional blueprint, on the basis of which the state was then created.

There is one major objection that may be made to this parallel I have drawn between the building of a house and the establishment of a state. The house is, clearly, a reality of the existential world: you can touch it, you can see it, you can photograph it; it has physical being. But you cannot see the United States of America as such, any more than you can see religious freedom as such. You cannot see the state, or touch it, as you can see and touch the house. There is physical territory which we identify with the United States of America. There are woods and fields, houses and roads, cities and towns—but these are not the state. They were there before the state was created and would still be there if the state were abolished tomorrow. Not being, in itself, a physical entity, the state does not, like the house, belong to the existential world. It belongs to the conceptual world.

Where, then, does the existential world come in? For our theme, after all, is man's role as a creator whose conceptual creation has its final form in the existential world.

I think we can best see how the existential world comes in by regarding the Constitution of the United States as the script of a play. Let us say that a playwright called 'Shakespeare' writes a play called *Hamlet*. That play has various parts or roles: a King (Claudius), a Queen (Gertrude), a Prince (Hamlet), a Lord Chamberlain (Polonius), Citizens, etc. The play is a nominal document, its parts nominal parts. Along come some existential men, however, in the guise of professional actors. They walk out onto the stage and severally proceed to act out the parts in accordance with the script. One assumes the role of the King and does what the King is supposed to do; another of the Queen – and so forth. Here the existential world imitates the conceptual world, the physical movements and speech of the actors following the script of the play as the physical building follows the blueprint.

The Constitution says: There shall be 'a President of the United States of America. He shall hold his Office during the Term of four Years, and . . . be elected as follows . . .' The procedure for his election is then prescribed. Along comes an actor called John F. Kennedy. He goes through the prescribed procedure, whereupon he assumes the role of the President of the United States of America. In that role he follows the script of the Constitution, essentially as the actor who takes the role of the King in *Hamlet* follows Shakespeare's script. For example, the Constitution says that the President of the United States of America 'shall nominate, and by and with the Advice and Consent of the Senate, shall appoint Ambassadors, other public Ministers and Consuls, Judges of the supreme Court . . .,' etc. So the actor who takes the part, in this case John F. Kennedy, proceeds to nominate and appoint ambassadors, other public ministers and consuls, judges of the Supreme Court . . ., etc.

This John F. Kennedy is only one actor in the existential performance of the script called, 'The Constitution of

43

the United States of America.' I, myself, am another. The role I play is a lesser one, that of a Citizen. The Constitution sets forth certain rights and certain duties of citizens. In my role as a Citizen, then, I exercise those rights and I discharge those duties.

The state is a concept, like the state to which More gave the name 'Utopia.' The Constitution is the nominal expression of this concept, like More's book, *Utopia*. But it is a live performance that we existential actors give of it, a performance in the existential world.

So we see the whole process of political creation, from the concept in the minds of existential men like Thomas Jefferson, to the communication of that concept in a script called 'The Constitution of the United States of America,' to its acting out by existential men in the existential world.

*   *   *

We are concerned with the relationship between the two disparate worlds in which we live out our whole lives, their relevance to each other. In the process of creation, the conceptual world comes first and the existential world imitates it. The conceptual world, however, is bound to bear in some degree the reciprocal impress of the existential.

We have seen that there may be an indefinitely great gap or virtually none at all between the original concept and its rendering in the existential world. Plato's concept of the ideal state was never actually enacted. Parts of More's concept were enacted centuries later. The concept set forth in the Constitution of the United States was enacted forthwith.

An architect does not ordinarily go out and construct the building he has conceived with his own hands. He sets forth his concept in the form of certain documents: drawings and lists of specifications. The matter might rest at that point. The architect might simply publish his documents for people to read and examine. This kind of thing is not unknown.

Mr. Hugh Ferriss, an American architect, used to publish drawings of imaginary buildings in imaginary cities of the future. These cities of the future were Utopias, like Sir Thomas More's, not intended for immediate realization in the existential world. But they may have had their influence on actual building in America, just as More's *Utopia* presumably had its influence on actual statecraft in England.

The man who makes drawings of an imaginary city of the future does not have to limit himself, in any strict sense, to what is possible or practicable in the excessively limited world of existential reality. On the other hand, the man who makes drawings for a building that it is proposed to erect forthwith does have to confine himself within such limits.

There have been playwrights who have written plays intended for reading only, rather than for actual production on the stage. (Goethe's *Faust* is an example.) This gives them a freedom from the limitations of existential reality, from the requirements of stagecraft in the existential world, that they would not otherwise have. Sometimes, when I have had to suffer through the attempted performance of an impossible work of symphonic music, I have later been told by professional musicians that it was what they call 'music for paper only.' That is to say, a trained musician might get pleasure out of reading the score because of the interest of daring or outlandish devices that it contains, but actual performance should never be attempted.

Sir Thomas More, because he did not intend his *Utopia* to be realized within the limits of the existential world as he knew it in his day, had the more freedom to indulge his idealism. In this instance, he accepted the gap between his conceptual world and the existential world, not pretending that his concepts could be given effect forthwith in the existential world. The authors of the Constitution of the United States did not have the same freedom, since they were producing the blueprint for a state to be set up forthwith.

That blueprint had to imitate the existential world to the extent of representing its possibilities and limits.

The authors of the Constitution faced the great dilemma of mankind in a more immediate and poignant sense than did Plato or Sir Thomas More. They had ideal models in their heads, but they had to corrupt those models, they had to make them less ideal, in order to adapt them to the existential scene. The history of the Constitutional Convention that met in Philadelphia in 1787 is the history of that agonizing procedure.

Surely the fault of the Dominican Constitution, modeled on that of the United States, was that it did not go far enough to meet the primitive existential circumstances of a society far less developed than that of the United States. The Dominican people were not sufficiently educated to act the roles which it assigned them. Hence the extreme disparity between the nominal model and the actual practice of Generalissimo Trujillo's government. The disparity is manifested everywhere and always, but generally not on such a scale. Where there is social progress it tends to diminish with time.

When the script of the Constitution of the United States had finally been adopted for performance in the existential world, and when the performance got under way, the gap between the two worlds was manifested by inevitable inadequacies in the performance. The Constitution itself, although the principal document embodying the design for the new state, was not the only such document. There were, for example, the constitutions of the several constituent states, and there was the *Declaration of Independence*, which set forth the philosophy and the principles on which the new state was to be based. One of the principles, represented as a self-evident truth, was 'that all men are created equal, that they are endowed by their creator with certain unalienable rights, that among these are life, liberty, and the pursuit of happiness.'

In nominal terms, then, all men without exception were to be regarded as equals and to be allowed the enjoyment of liberty. How can one reconcile this nominal situation with the institutionalized inequality of Negroes, and their servitude, in the new state?

The answer is that one cannot altogether reconcile them. They represent the eternal gap between the two worlds, in this case the gap between the script and its existential enactment.

I repeat, however, that where there is social progress the gap tends to diminish with time. At first there was a typical confusion. What the Founding Fathers may have had chiefly in mind, when the *Declaration of Independence* was drafted, was their long-standing demand that all Englishmen receive equal treatment. They were outraged by the metropolitan government's policy of keeping the Englishmen who lived in America in a status inferior to that of the Englishmen who lived in England. At a level closer to practical affairs, more remote from ideal concepts, what they had in mind was that all *Englishmen* are created equal and are endowed by their creator with certain unalienable rights, among which are life, liberty, and the pursuit of happiness. One may doubt that they were thinking of Hottentots, for example.

However, even leaving aside basic Christian doctrine, rhetorical considerations, which are considerations bearing on what binds the nominal to the ideal, require great principles to be cast in general terms. Otherwise they will lack the moral authority of ideal concepts. The *Declaration of Independence* would have lost moral authority if it had proclaimed the equality of all men and their right to liberty — with the exception of those who were not English. So the Founding Fathers, omitting any fine print, simply proclaimed the equality of all men and the right of all to liberty. In the state that was then set up on the basis of this principle, however, Negroes were tacitly excluded from its benefits.

The actors refrained from a literal interpretation of a script that was not, presumably, intended to be taken literally.

In 1857, in connection with the Dred Scott Case, the Supreme Court of the United States decided: that Negroes, whether slave or free, were not, and could not be, citizens of the United States of America; that Negro slaves constituted private property, in the possession of which the owners should be protected by the government. Existential Negroes, in other words, were not to act the part of Citizen in the performance of the play; they were to act the part of Private Property.[3]

This decision of the Supreme Court, however, outraged a large part of the American citizenry—outraged them precisely because it appeared to them irreconcilable with the nominal terms of the ideal concept on which they had been brought up. This influence of the ideal concept, through the general terms used in its nominal expression, led in a few years to the outbreak of the Civil War, to the freeing of the slaves, to the abolition of slavery by the Thirteenth Amendment of the Constitution, to the establishment of the citizenship of Negroes and ex-slaves in the Fourteenth Amendment, and to the Fifteenth Amendment, which provided that 'the right of citizens of the United States to vote shall not be denied or abridged by the United States or any State on account of race, color, or previous condition of servitude.'

So, in time, the world of ideal concepts comes to prevail over the existential world. So, in time, the word is made flesh.

[3] Huckleberry Finn, in Mark Twain's novel of that name, undergoes an agonizing inner conflict when he finds himself helping Jim escape from slavery. He is torn between the concept of Jim as a fellow man and the concept of Jim as the private property of Miss Watson, who had never done him any harm. See Chapters 16 and 31 of the novel.

Chapter 3

THE NECESSITY OF MEDIATION

WE began by noting that international relations as practiced are one thing, as taught another. Consideration of the difference led us to make a distinction between two worlds, the existential and the conceptual. This is the distinction between an aboriginal chaos and an order in our minds to which we try to make that chaos conform.

In the absence of any imposed order from the conceptual world, the chaos of the existential world is absolute. As for the conceptual world, men have always supposed that there was an absolute order, somehow preceding the existential world, and self-contained. In *Genesis* the absolute chaos is represented by the earth as it was in the beginning, 'without form and void'; the absolute order by 'the Spirit of God.' In the Fourth Gospel, the absolute order is represented by the Logos, the Word that was in the beginning. A teleological view would see us today as midway in a process of establishing the order of the Logos over the chaos that was in the beginning. At this stage of development, an order that is only partial has been imposed on a chaos that is only partially vanquished.[1]

Although we may believe in the absolute order represented by the Logos, we do not, for the most part, know what that order is. We cannot see it whole, whatever intimations of it may come to us. Such particular concepts of order as we are able to evoke or produce in our limited minds remain incomplete and imperfect. Even so, we find it necessary to

---

[1] Teleological views are out of fashion, as are any views that postulate the existence of something beyond what is knowable to us by scientific evidence. The thesis of these chapters, however, does not in the least depend on such views.

corrupt them so that they may be susceptible of application within the limits of an existential world that is still so largely chaotic. The man who conceives the design of a state intended for realization in the existential circumstances of his time and place finds that, to make it applicable, he has to renounce its ideal aspects.

The conceptual world of our minds may be represented by a spectrum that extends from something approaching a perfect order, at one end, to the brink of chaos at the other. The difference between the professors of utopian tendency described in the first chapter and the practitioners in the State Department is not that the former live in the conceptual world while the latter live in the existential world. Both live in the conceptual world, since that is the only world of the mind; but, because the practitioners are at closer grips with the existential circumstances that have to be ordered, their conceptions respond more to the criterion of applicability, and less to abstract ideals, than do those of the professors. The practitioner stands at the brink of chaos, trying to manage it directly, like the man at the wheel of the ship who is preoccupied with the towering waves that charge toward the prow. The professor is like the navigator, less involved in what is immediate, therefore able to take a longer view. The longer the view, the less urgent the question of applicability; the less urgent the question of applicability, the less the need to compromise with whatever may happen to be his ideal. In the longest view, no compromise is needed at all, the question of applicability becomes so remote as to be irrelevant.

I have no doubt that the world has work to do for utopians and practical operators alike, as well as for those who fall between the extremes. Every ship needs a hand at the wheel. It also needs, among its officers, at least one who is able to think beyond the moment in terms of a course to be followed. The place where the course of a ship begins, however, as it moves toward the future, is always *here*, and the time *now*.

Therefore, an officer who plots courses only in remote oceans of the imagination, to which the ship may someday come, will be of limited use. He may be a nuisance if he insists that his directions should be accepted for immediate application.

Two elements are indispensable for statesmanship. One is vision, which is the ability to see beyond the transient circumstances of the immediate present. The other is the discipline of responsibility, which prevents the statesman from overlooking the limits set by the circumstances of the immediate present. True statesmanship performs a mediating function. It performs that function in a zone of tension between a large conceptual order on the one hand and, on the other, the existential circumstances that resist the imposition of that order. To accept the circumstances as they are would be to embrace chaos. But to uphold an ideal order in contempt of those circumstances would be to close one's eyes to the basic dilemma with which life challenges us. It would be to evade the burden of resolving that dilemma by refusing to recognize that it exists.

We manage our problems more intelligently, and with greater mutual understanding, when we can bring ourselves to recognize them as expressions of mankind's basic dilemma. In politics especially, they do not confront us with simple choices between right and wrong, between good and evil (as the polemical terms in which politics are conducted would have us believe). Although we all agree in identifying the original chaos of the existential world with evil, we still cannot escape its requirements. The necessity of evil, then, is the dilemma. Only those who do not bear the direct burden of responsibility for decision and action can indulge themselves in the denial of that necessity. Abraham Lincoln, in his Emancipation Proclamation, excepted from enfranchisement the slaves of certain political groups who would otherwise have withheld their support from him. His critics were surely right in saying that this was morally indefensible. What is morally indefensible may, however, be politically unavoidable. This is the dilemma. The better we understand it, the more charitable we shall be to those who bear the great political responsibilities.

> Bullfight critics ranked in rows
> Crowd the enormous plaza full;
> But only one is there who *knows*
> And he's the man who fights the bull.

The verse is by a Spanish bullfighter, Domingo Ortega, in Robert Graves's translation.[2] It was cited by President Kennedy in an informal talk to a small group in Washington at a time when he was faced with the most portentous decision of his career. The making of that decision provides an illustration of my point.

Beginning in November 1958, Soviet efforts to prize the Western allies out of Berlin, where they were committed to remain for the defense of the free Berliners, produced a series of crises that, on occasion, seemed to be sweeping the world toward a third world war. Locally, the military position of the Western allies was hopeless. Their token forces in Berlin were completely surrounded by territory under the control of overwhelmingly greater Communist forces. The only way Berlin could be defended was by the manifestation of a determination, on the part of the United States and its allies, to carry resistance to the point where a full-scale nuclear war might well break out—leaving the Soviets to decide whether they wanted to let matters go that far. The manifestation of this determination, in successive crises, was effective in deterring the Soviet Union from the ultimate challenge because it was backed by an American nuclear establishment believed capable of putting an end to the Soviet Union. The Soviet government could calculate, however, that the United States would be less likely to use this

[2] Published in *Encounter*, London, December 1961.

establishment for the defense of Berlin if the Soviet Union, by some kind of 'breakthrough,' could gain a greater known capability of retaliating on American cities.

Through the summer and early fall of 1962 there were indications that Moscow was preparing, for November, another attempt to force the United States and its allies out of Berlin. Presumably it would not simply repeat its earlier attempts, which had failed, but would bring some new element of pressure to bear. What this would be, no one knew.

Then, in the middle of October, American 'planes flying reconnaissance missions over Cuba discovered that Russian ballistic missiles, some with ranges up to two thousand miles, had suddenly been introduced into the island, and that their launching sites were being erected with the utmost speed. At the same time, Russian bombers designed for the delivery of nuclear weapons were being rushed into Cuba, and their take-off bases were also being made ready. All this work was proceeding so rapidly that, within a matter of days, the United States could expect to find itself confronting the accomplished fact of a Soviet nuclear base, just off its shores, capable of almost instantaneously destroying any of its Southern, Eastern, or Middle Western cities. All this was being done clandestinely, so as to effect surprise, under cover of explicit assurances from the top Soviet spokesmen to the President and other American officials that no such armament was being or would be introduced into Cuba.

It was not hard to see a connection between this sudden move, which must have been months in preparation, and the expected move against Berlin in November. The nuclear base in Cuba would represent the 'breakthrough' Moscow needed. It would abruptly alter the relative power-positions of the Soviet Union and the United States. By its intimidating effect on the American public and the American government, it was bound to make the United States more cautious of taking risks for Berlin.

When this Soviet move was discovered, the time in which effective action might be taken to frustrate it was a matter of days. The question posed for the President was what action to take.

A nominal model for the action to be taken by any member of the international community in such a contingency was available. There was a script to be acted out. International law and international agreements, including the Charter of the United Nations, prescribed that, when any nation became aware of a threat to international peace, it was to bring that threat to the attention of the Security Council of the United Nations, which would then assume the responsibility for dealing with it.

How would the Security Council go about dealing with it?

The script prescribed that too. The Security Council would decide what action to take by a majority vote of its members, including the unanimous vote of its five permanent members. Since the Soviet Union was one of the five, that would enable it to veto any effective action.

In 1950 a possible way around an impasse in the Security Council had been provided by the so-called 'United Action for Peace' resolution, passed by the General Assembly of the United Nations. This provided that, if and when the Security Council failed to exercise its responsibility for the maintenance of international peace and security, a meeting of the General Assembly might be called on twenty-four hours' notice. The Charter did not give the General Assembly any such powers for dealing with threats to the peace as it conferred on the Security Council. However, by a two-thirds vote of its members (totalling 108 at the time of the Cuban crisis), the General Assembly could give moral support to what individual nations might do on their own, or in combination with others, to meet a threat of aggression. In other words, if two-thirds of the members chose, they could give some aura of legitimacy to actions that were, perhaps, outside the letter, if not the spirit of the law.

No one could doubt that, by the time all the procedures provided for in the script had been gone through, any action by the international organization would come too late. The Soviet nuclear base in Cuba would have already become an established fact, and a crisis over Berlin might be holding the world in suspense. What, in any case, could the General Assembly do about a Soviet nuclear base in Cuba? What would it do? The point of these questions needs no elaboration.

The President of the United States was in the position of a bullfighter in the ring who, faced with a particularly menacing charge by the bull, knows that he will end up on the bull's horns if he meets that charge by the ideal action which the book of rules prescribes for such contingencies. Although the President did have the matter placed before the Security Council with the utmost urgency, this in itself was not enough.

What else was there for him to do?

According to the rules, a nation might not, on its own, take military action against another nation except if it was doing so in self-defense against an overt aggression. It might not even impose a blockade. What the rule-book said, in effect, was that, when a man's sworn enemy puts a pistol to his head, he may act on his own to defend himself only if and when the pistol is fired.

For six days, after the Government of the United States had discovered and confirmed what was going on in Cuba, it maintained silence while it decided what to do. Then, on the evening of October 22, the President, in a broadcast, announced to the world the construction of the Soviet base in Cuba, and the introduction of Soviet missiles. Noting that 'we no longer live in a world where only the actual firing of weapons represents a sufficient challenge to a nation's security to constitute a maximum peril,' he said that, among the

government's objectives in dealing with the situation, was
that of securing the 'withdrawal or elimination' of the missiles
from the Western Hemisphere. Toward this end, it was asking for an emergency meeting of the Security Council to
take action against the 'threat to world peace.' It was not,
however, confining itself to this. The President said that he
had already ordered a naval blockade of Cuba (which, in
deference to the prohibition of peacetime 'blockade' by international law, he called a 'quarantine') in order to prevent
any more 'offensive military equipment' from reaching Cuba.
'All ships of any kind bound for Cuba, from whatever nation
or port, will, if found to contain cargoes of offensive weapons,
be turned back.' He added a clear threat that, if this did not
prove effective in accomplishing the objective, then the armed
forces of the United States would, if necessary, invade Cuba
to accomplish it. Finally, he held out an olive-branch to the
Soviet Union, urging a general settlement of the Cold War,
and the establishment of amicable relations, after the withdrawal of the missiles from Cuba.

On October 28, after direct correspondence back and
forth between President Kennedy and Premier Khrushchev,
the latter agreed to withdraw the missiles and to dismantle
their launching sites. As was a foregone conclusion, the
Security Council had done nothing. One should add, however, that informal behind-the-scenes actions at United
Nations Headquarters (*i.e.*, actions that were not based on
the forms prescribed in the Charter) made an important
contribution to the resolution of the crisis.

In the months that preceded the crisis and led up to it,
public opinion in England, as it was represented by a major
part of the British press, had shown an increasing desire to
dissociate England from her involvement in the Cold War,
in which she was the principal ally of the United States. This
desire had its expression in an unconsciously motivated tendency to regard the United States and what it stood for as

hardly less alien to England than the Soviet Union and what it stood for. Americans were made to appear outlandish and irresponsible, and any strange or menacing aspects of Soviet behavior were played down. By the time of the Cuban crisis, then, most of the big English newspapers were dealing with the Cold War as a contest between two alien giants, both foreign to Britain, whose position was referred to as if it was that of a detached spectator in danger of becoming involved in a fight that was not his own.

In the days before President Kennedy's dramatic address on October 22, the opinion became general in England that he was about to launch an invasion of Cuba, not for any sound strategic reason, but simply to gain votes for his party in the national elections that were less than a month away. Commentators who should have known better began to cry out in alarm at the prospect, as they saw it, that a nuclear war in which Britain would be annihilated was about to be risked by the Kennedy Administration for reasons of American domestic politics. The British public, quite distinct from the British government in this, was too far from the seat of responsibility to be disciplined by the realism that responsibility imposes, to feel its sobering effect, or even to credit the sobriety of those who bore its burden. In any case, they had fed themselves too long on the wildness and iniquity of Americans.

Under the circumstances, the immediate reaction of perhaps a majority of the important British newspapers to the President's broadcast of October 22 was that it confirmed their worst fears. The Soviet Union and Cuba were being directly menaced, and the rest of the world was being indirectly menaced, by a reckless, aggressive action which Washington was timing to influence the forthcoming elections.[3]

[3] The reader will find a circumstantial account of the British press and the Cuban crisis in the issue of the British magazine *Encounter* for January

When the crisis ended, on a remarkably gentle note, in agreement and cooperation between the United States and the Soviet Union, the British press responded with second thoughts that were, in several instances, magnanimous. What many Englishmen could not forgive, however, was that the government in Washington had flouted the procedures prescribed by international law. Leaving existential realities out of account, the formal situation was clear, and it bore them out. The Soviet Union had in no way violated international law by undertaking to make Cuba a base for nuclear weapons. The United States, on the other hand, had violated international law by instituting a blockade in peacetime, and had flouted the United Nations by taking action without awaiting a decision by the Security Council.

At the time, I had occasion to make a public comment, in England, in which, noting that much of the British press had criticized the American action by the standards of the world as it should be, I asked for tolerance on the grounds that 'responsibility has to be discharged in the world as it is.' This brought me a fusillade of letters claiming that, not only had the authority of international law been damaged, but the United Nations had been dealt such a blow by the American action that it might never recover.

What is particularly worth noting is that these letters did not come from that part of the population which had been least exposed to a formal education in international relations. They came from intellectuals, and they came notably from those who had sat at the feet of my fellow professors in an earlier generation, learning from them to regard the existential reality of the world as an unnecessary aberration from the world as it should be, an aberration attributable to the

1963 (pp. 84–95) and in Part I ('Cuba Week') of John Mander's *Great Britain or Little England*, London, 1963. For the most sober and responsible expression of the neutralist psychology that was developing before the Cuban crisis, and that I have described here, see the editorials in *The Observer* through the late summer and early autumn of 1962.

narrow and greedy outlook of politicians. (The habit of attributing all blame for the world's ills to the villainy of politicians and people in government was what enabled them to believe, in the words of the London *Tribune* during the crisis, 'that Kennedy is risking blowing the world to hell in order to sweep a few Democrats into office . . .') One who had belonged to a former generation of students at the Graduate Institute of International Studies in Geneva, where I teach, wrote me, 'as one who loved and admired' my predecessors on the faculty 'precisely for their rooted ideals,' that he was 'saddened by your appeal to *Realpolitik*, coming as it does with the *cachet* of the Institute's address.'

It makes it much more difficult [he continued], to keep the actions of governments within the compass of international rules and their obligations in the humdrum little things which make up the community of nations when, on these major issues someone in your position supports the illegal use of force. . . . The case for trying to dish the other fellow regardless of the rules is easy enough to see. Support for the law is the difficult, not the easy, course.

I cite this typical letter because it represents a paradox that bears on my point. This correspondent had less understanding of the Cuban crisis than if he had never studied international relations at all, since he had studied them in terms of contempt for the world as it is. Taught to believe that the world is what it is, not by any inherent necessity, but by the accident that short-sighted or unscrupulous politicians hold power in it, he thought of the choices that confront governments as simple choices between right and wrong.

Another correspondent wrote me that 'the American action over Cuba has dealt a possibly mortal blow to the U.N.'; and this was the more tragic, he held, because the U.N. would have been so strengthened, and the worldwide rule of law so advanced, if the United States had acted in accordance with the rules.

Such a conclusion is indisputable if one confines one's

thinking to an abstract logic that leaves existential circumstances out of account. Law and international organization,
according to this logic, gain authority where they are re-
spected, lose authority where they are flouted: having been
flouted by the United States, they must have lost authority.
However, if one takes account of the existential world, ad-
ventitious factors enter in that may overset this logic, valid
as it is in itself, to produce the opposite conclusion. (One
will generally misjudge political phenomena, in which transient or accidental factors play such a dominant role, if one
surrenders oneself to an abstract logic conceived to represent
an *a priori* truth, no matter how beautiful that logic or how
much it obviates the strains and uncertainties that must
otherwise bedevil the mind.)

Taking existential circumstances into account, it was predictable that the Soviet Union would veto any action by the
Security Council to make it abandon its project in Cuba. It
was predictable that the General Assembly would not have
been able, even if willing, to make good the default of the
Security Council. The Soviet missile-base would have been
firmly established in Cuba, and it is likely that the next
Soviet move would have been against Berlin. No one can tell
what would have happened after that, but it is not unlikely
that a situation similar to that in Europe during the winter
of 1938–9 would have ensued—with a series of crises cul-
minating in all-out disaster.

I cannot believe that, if the President had stuck to the
rules, the United Nations and international law would, in
fact, have been strengthened. What the President faced was
not a simple choice between right and wrong but a dilemma
involving the necessity of evil. His job was to choose the
lesser evil and reject the greater.

The United Nations might truly have been damaged if
it had been called on to undertake a task beyond its means,
a task in which its ineffectiveness was made plain for all to

see. As it was, so far from being damaged by the American action, it gained in prestige from the part its secretariat played in bringing about a successful resolution of the crisis. More than that, the successful resolution produced an international atmosphere more conducive to the rule of law and the operations of international organization than had been known for a generation. It produced, almost immediately, a relaxation of international tensions and a notable abatement of the Cold War. Moscow, having tested the West and found it firm, evidently came to the conclusion that it would rather be on better than on worse terms with it. If there is any lesson to be learned from international history since the middle of the last century, when the increasing weakness of China and of Turkey produced an increasing deterioration in the international situation, it is that excessive weakness at any key point in the structure of world equilibrium is productive of chaos. International stability depends on the solidity of its constituent elements. The resolution of the Cuban crisis, I conclude, averted a proliferation of chaos that would have been inimical to the development of international law and international organization.

Looking only at the *a priori* model, averting their eyes from the claims of the existential world, my correspondents escaped the anguish of facing the real dilemma. Not having the responsibility, they could refuse to recognize the necessity of evil, thereby clothing themselves in an outward virtue that made them shine by contrast with those who did have the responsibility.

If I am driving my car along the highway, an occasion might arise in which I was confronted with the alternatives of crossing the white line in the center or hitting a pedestrian. The white line represents the law that I must not transgress; the pedestrian is an existential circumstance that, let us suppose, should not have been on the highway at all. Faced with a choice of evils, either to break the law or hit the pedestrian, most of us would choose to cross the white line, violating a general principle out of regard for an accidental circumstance. Would it be altogether right, then, to denounce us for showing a contempt of the law? In the world as it should have been, there would have been no need to cross the white line (since the pedestrian would not have been there), but our responsibility required us to act on the basis of the world as it was.

Let me put the matter in other terms. In the existential world, dogs often show themselves hostile and dangerous to passing pedestrians. Imagine, now, a man who avows the belief that, if a pedestrian only shows a friendly disposition toward a hostile dog, the dog will drop his hostility and reciprocate the friendliness that he senses in the pedestrian. If the dog was initially hostile, our man claims, it was because he assumed and anticipated hostility, rather than love, on the part of the pedestrian. The man who holds such a belief but remains indoors will find it easy to criticize a pedestrian whom he observes through the window defending himself against an attacking dog. He may point out that the pedestrian could have avoided the attack by showing himself friendly to the dog in the first instance. The real test of the observer, and of his theory, however, comes only when he finds himself out on the street and being approached by a big dog who growls and bares his fangs. At that moment it may be borne in on him for the first time that the existential dog cannot be counted on to react as simply and surely as the conceptual dog—if only because the element of accident now enters in. The situation begins to appear more complex and uncertain. The gap between the conceptual and existential worlds becomes important. The gap between the world as it should be and the world as it is becomes important. The observer suddenly finds himself having to act in the world as it is.

I recall how, in the 1930's, there were those who maintained that, if only Hitler were dealt with in a friendly way, if only he were not provoked by defensive and suspicious reactions, if only he were not antagonized by the rearmament of those who allowed themselves to view him with fear and hostility—then he would not hurt anybody. Some held that he would respond to love with love. So far from having contempt for this view, it seems to me to represent a fundamental truth. But only a partial truth. The ideal conditions in which it might work would probably not be matched by the actual conditions in which it would have to be applied. Therefore it was more easily held by those who did not have the direct responsibility for decision than by those who did.

We have the example of Mr. Jawaharlal Nehru, the Prime Minister of India. For years, looking out of the window at the Western Powers in the street, he admonished them against constituting themselves a 'power-bloc,' against playing 'power politics,' against arming themselves with terrible weapons. Looking across his own frontiers at Communist China, he based his government's policy on the belief that, if he showed a friendly and unsuspicious attitude, it would be reciprocated. China would not bite him. So his government refrained from erecting effective defenses along the Chinese border. Then, however, at the same time as the Cuban crisis in the West, China bit him. In a series of massive military attacks, it did not resist the temptation to overrun the undefended Indian frontier. Since then, India has been building up her defenses as best she can, and has been responding with hostility to the hostility of the Chinese. The gap between Mr. Nehru's conceptual world and the existential world was too great. Consequently, he had to modify his concepts to make them conform more closely to existential circumstances as he found them to be.

In teaching international relations it would be impossible to teach only the world as it is. Ideal models are the proper subject of teaching. But it would be wrong to present them as immediate alternatives to the world as it is. It would be wrong to teach them in terms that represented the task of statesmanship as that of choosing between good and evil, rather than as that of mediating between two worlds, both of which have their claims. We ought to teach ideal models in terms of the strict limits that existential circumstances impose on their applicability at any particular time and place. Otherwise we might raise new generations that, blind to anything except an abstract and *a priori* good, would with the best intentions bring the greatest evils upon us.

The illustration of this danger is the burden of the next four chapters.

PART TWO

Which illustrates the tragic consequences of an excessive divergence between the two worlds by citing the history of a modern ideology.

Chapter 4

THE ROAD TO MARXISM

AT the end of the eighteenth century, and through the beginning of the nineteenth, the civilization of Europe was swept by a storm that tore the societies of the day from their traditional moorings. The French Revolution and the subsequent campaigns of the French citizen-armies under Napoleon were not, themselves, prime causes. European civilization was already beginning to be transformed by the industrial revolution, which was dissolving the hierarchy of classes that had developed under feudalism, which would create urban concentrations on a scale previously unknown, and which would entail the various developments associated with mass culture. The French Revolution, however, epitomized all this. When it had passed away, people looked out on a new landscape. In spite of putative 'restorations,' the dominant class was no longer the cultivated aristocracy but the *nouveau-riche* bourgeoisie. The men whose business was money held the citadels of civilization; their wives, ambitious to appear high-class and respectable, set the tone. The vulgarity caricatured by Honoré Daumier in France was everywhere in the ascendent. The decay of the aristocracy, the callousness of the middle classes, and the degradation of the urban poor, combined to present a sordid spectacle. Sensitive persons naturally rebelled against it. Refusing to identify themselves with the society in which they lived, they formed an 'alienated' class in its midst.

The alienation of the individual, as such, took the form of romanticism. Already in the middle of the eighteenth century, in Jean-Jacques Rousseau, we see this romantic alienation full-blown. The romantic, turning away from the harsh outer world, looks inward and becomes preoccupied

67

with his own sensitive soul. The standard drama of life is that of the individual against society, the individual being oneself. Creation becomes self-expression. The artist paints for himself (paints his own vision rather than the stuff around him), preferring rather to starve in his garret than sell his soul for the rewards of middle-class respectability. Novelists and poets write *pour épater le bourgeois*. Young Werther has his sorrows. The Lady of the Camellias languishes and fades and finally passes away from a world that has been too cruel. Composers write symphonic autobiographies, relating the successive states of their own souls: first youthful hope, then disillusion and bitterness, and in the finale a noble resignation.[1]

The new alienation also found its expression in an important new profession. From 1815 until well on in the twentieth century, professional revolutionaries made their careers out of working for the abrupt replacement of existing social systems by ideal systems of their own conception. There were anarchists like Bakunin and Kropotkin; republicans like Mazzini; socialists of one sort or another, like Blanqui, Marx, Kautsky; syndicalists like Georges Sorel. Regarding themselves as alienated from the existing society, they set themselves to organize warfare against it. Some were disposed to believe that the overthow of that society would be

---

[1] Moses Hess, whom we shall come upon later in this chapter, in a typical romantic gesture married a prostitute–'in order to atone for the evil society had done.' The tendency of the romantics was to idealize prostitutes because they were outcasts from polite society.

Compare Shakespeare's sonnet-sequence with the one Edna St. Vincent Millay wrote on the same pattern in the twentieth century, called *Fatal Interview*. Both are almost embarrassingly personal, relating the history of the authors' love-affairs. No poet, not even Shakespeare, has commanded language as beautiful as that of *Fatal Interview*. But there is a fundamental contrast. Shakespeare's sonnets are focussed on the superior qualities of the one he loves, which make him feel his own unworthiness. Miss Millay's celebrate the quality of her own feelings and are quite clear on the unworthiness of the ordinary mortal whom she honors with them. Miss Millay's life was a sustained expression of indignation at an unworthy world.

virtually enough in itself to produce the good life for man-kind. Others were entranced by various conceptions of an ideal society that could be brought into being only after the existing society had been got out of the way. These ideologists sat about in the cafés of Paris, Brussels, Geneva, or Zürich, or in the rooming-houses of London, arguing endlessly, writing pamphlets and manifestos, drawing up resolutions, organizing and planning, conspiring against one another as often as against outsiders. They were homeless, they were familiar with the insides of jails, they were generally hard-up; but they were sustained by a sense of mission that en-abled them to endure poverty and insecurity without repin-ing. They thought of themselves as the rescuers of mankind; they thought of themselves as the locomotives of history; they thought of themselves as the midwives of the final age of man, the age of human fulfilment that was about to be born. (It just missed being born in 1848.)

One may doubt that most of these professional revolution-aries were intellectually impressive. Alienated from the actual societies of their day, they were living almost wholly in worlds of fantasy. Men who, perhaps, had never seen a Russian peasant, recruited the whole mass of them into revolutionary armies of the imagination. Intellectuals who had never had any contact with factory-workers undertook to be their spokesmen and contributed them to the cause. Over the café tables they maneuvered the armies of the European powers, parceled out provinces, and set empire against empire. Only their extreme intellectual intensity, and their lack of self-doubt, gave plausibility to their pretensions.

This rag-tag and bobtail of revolutionaries ranged from bomb-throwing adventurers to men of powerful and dis-tinguished intellect. It is clear today that the outstanding example of the latter was a German of essentially academic background, Dr. Heinrich Karl Marx.

* * *

When we first meet, close up and in informal circumstances, anyone whom we have learned to regard as a 'great man,' we are always disappointed. This is because there is no such thing as a 'great man' in the existential world. The 'great man' known to the public is a conceptual figure abstracted from the existential man with whom one shakes hands. I suppose that Karl Marx, arguing with other left-wing intellectuals in a café on the Galeries Saint-Hubert in Brussels, appeared as one shabby young man among the others. His friend, Friedrich Engels, would one day be ironically amused at the myth of this same Karl Marx as it was blown up, after his death, by the rather silly revolutionaries of the younger generation.

What did this man have that made him, at last, such a powerful influence in history? As a revolutionary, organizing revolutionary action, he was no better than others of his day. He was to go in for economics later, basing his thought on the classical and rather naïve labor theory of value, but it was not as an economist that he would achieve the topmost heights of distinction. As a political analyst he was surely not as good as his contemporary of lesser fame, Walter Bagehot; as a social philosopher he was inferior to Alexis de Tocqueville. His development of the sociological view that men's concepts reflect the material circumstances of their productive lives—this certainly would entitle him to an important place in the history of human thought. But it is hardly commensurate with the magnitude of his influence.

Marx was extraordinary, I conclude, not as a man of action or as an academic thinker, but as one of the great visionaries of history. It was the Karl Marx who saw an immense and enthralling vision of human society, the Karl Marx who on the basis of that vision created a compelling myth of human society—this is the Marx who was extraordinary among his contemporaries. He had more of St. Paul in him than of the social scientist or the empirical scholar.

As we shall see, his mission, too, began with a vision on the Road to Damascus.

Marx was a social philosopher who did not give himself altogether to the conspiratorial side of revolution. He appears to have been happiest in a library. He was not, like so many uneducated revolutionaries, without background. As a man of advanced education, who took his doctorate in philosophy at the University of Jena after studying at Bonn and Berlin, he stood in the van of the great philosophical tradition of his day, which was precisely the tradition that addressed itself to the problem of alienation.

To try to understand the philosophy of Marx as a self-contained body of thought is like trying to understand the fourth chapter of a book of which one has not read the first three. For Chapter One we have to go back at least to Immanuel Kant in the eighteenth century. After Kant had written the first chapter in this line of philosophical development, Georg Wilhelm Friedrich Hegel came along and wrote an additional chapter of such intrinsic power that he thereby gave his name to the whole tradition of German philosophy from that point on. Those who came after him were ostensibly commentators on the chapter he had written, calling themselves Hegelians or neo-Hegelians or post-Hegelians, Old Hegelians or Young Hegelians. Ludwig Feuerbach transformed Hegelianism, and then Marx transformed Feuerbach's transformation. Philosophy had become a matter of writing glosses on Hegel and glosses on glosses of Hegel, of interpreting him and interpreting the interpretations until Hegel would have been surprised at what bore the name of 'Hegelianism,' even if hyphenated with other terms. When Marx studied at the Universities of Bonn, Berlin, and Jena, the philosophy he studied was Hegelianism. Indeed, at Berlin the memory of Professor Hegel's lectures was still fresh.

Judaism and Christianity had been based on the concept

of two worlds, the perfect and the imperfect. God represented perfection; man, made in his image, had fallen into imperfection. When Jesus came to redeem mankind, he provided the example of Godlike perfection on which men were to model themselves.[2]

A sophisticated version of this duality is represented by the philosophy of Kant. The two worlds are the phenomenal world, which is the world known to our faculties of perception (*i.e.*, the world of appearances that are not necessarily true representations of reality), and the noumenal world, the world of 'things in themselves' (*i.e.*, the world of realities that we cannot apprehend because our faculties of perception present us with appearances only). Phenomenal man is the

[2] From here on I depend heavily on Robert C. Tucker, *Philosophy and Myth in Karl Marx*, Cambridge, 1961, a book that makes clear much that would otherwise remain obscure. It has been attacked on doctrinal grounds by those who, while opposed to what the Soviet Union represents as Marxism, revere Marx as an empirical scientist, the Darwin of social science. (*E.g.*, T. B. Bottomore, in *Karl Marx: Early Writings*, London, 1963, p. xii.) The magic of Marx's appeal still arouses, a century later, a passionate defense against those whose criticism tends to diminish his intellectual authority. In truth, however, one could quote, endlessly, passages of Marx that no one could reconcile with the statement that the cast of his mind was 'fundamentally scientific.' (Aside from the passages of evident myth-making, I raise the question whether the famous statement with which he ends his *Theses on Feuerbach*, that the point is not to interpret but to change the world, is to be reconciled with scientific detachment.) On the other hand, much of *Capital* does represent scientific method and scientific apparatus. It is only a narrow view of our human nature that will not allow the possibility of scientific activities by a myth-maker or of mythical proclivities by a scientist.

For a moving and deeply felt example of what remains, nevertheless, hagiography, see Erich Fromm in *Marx's Concept of Man*, New York, 1961. Fromm is at least as incensed against the Bolsheviks who betrayed Marx's Marxism as against those who today make him out to have been a demonic monster, which he certainly was not. If Tucker fails to present him as a god, however, neither does he present him as any kind of a monster. Surely there can be no adequate Marxian scholarship as long as scholars tend to be preoccupied with the question of being either for or against Marx!

A substantial part of what follows in this and the next chapter is essentially a summary of matters set forth by Professor Tucker. He and the Cambridge University Press have kindly given me their permission to do this.

slave of a causal system that represents predetermination. By contrast, noumenal man, whom we have to take on faith, is free. Our noumenal selves, by contrast with our phenomenal selves, are subject to a morality that necessarily has freedom as one of its premises.

In terms of this philosophical system, the individual finds himself involved in an 'antinomy' or contradiction: the contradiction between the predetermined causality to which his apparent self is subject and the moral freedom that his real self enjoys. After Kant, this distinction between the two selves, with its implications of inner conflict, comes to be regarded as intolerable. The duality must be overcome, wholeness must be achieved.

In Hegel's philosophy—and this explains the appeal it had—it *is* overcome, wholeness *is* achieved. All being is basically one and indivisible. It is what Hegel calls 'the Absolute Idea.' We can call it 'God' (or 'mind' or 'spirit' or 'thought thinking itself'). The reality of man, in this monistic conception, is not distinguishable from the reality of God except in its lack of completion. Perfection can be realized only through the experience of imperfection, wholeness through the experience of partialness, good through the experience of evil. Therefore, God has become split, has lost his wholeness. He has, to put it in the language relevant to our theme, alienated himself in external objects, in external objects that represent his own self dismembered, so to speak. (Man is God become partial.) History is the process by which God, having alienated himself in external objects, progressively overcomes his alienation by acquiring knowledge of the external objects, thereby making them a part of his subjective self again. Since man is real only in his identification with the Absolute (God), this means that: the world of which man is conscious as being external to himself, as being an objective world, represents his own alienated self (God's alienated self); by the process of coming to know it he makes it no longer alien, he comprehends it, he re-incorporates it in himself; and this process goes on until there is no longer a dual world of subject and object, until the entire alien world has been comprehended, has been overcome and absorbed, until all being is finally one—the universal God who is indistinguishable from the human self; until all being is, more precisely, the Logos, for Hegel iden-tified being in its totality with the rational.

History, for Hegel, is the dialectical process by which God overcomes his alienation. Replace 'God' with 'Man' and this is what history is for Marx as well.

Alienation is better known to us, in the twentieth century, as a psychiatric rather than a philosophical term. It represents a common mental ailment. The alienated person loses his feeling of personal identity. Perhaps he identifies himself with the godlike image of himself, and so regards his exist-ential self as alien. He becomes a split personality—and when this splitting of the personality, this alienation, goes to an extreme, what you have is a case of severe neurosis. The cure that Hegel offers for this (for what he calls *Selbstentfremdung* or self-alienation) is knowledge. 'The aim of knowledge,' he says, 'is to divest the objective world that stands opposed to us of its strangeness, and, as the phrase is, to find ourselves at home in it: which means no more than to trace the objective world back to the notion—to our innermost self.'[3]

*   *   *

In the dual world of Hegel's philosophy, as in that of Plato, the spirit or the mind or the idea (God or the Logos) has primacy. It is the basic reality, and existential reality is the alienated matter that has to be re-assimilated by the

---

[3] Hegel, *The Logic of Hegel*, translated from *The Encyclopaedia of the Philosophical Sciences* by William Wallace. London, 1950, p. 335. (Quoted in Tucker, *op. cit.*, p. 49.)

dialectical process of coming to know it. This attribution of primacy to the idea was bound to come into direct collision with the positivism that was becoming predominant in the generation immediately after Hegel. For positivism regards only the existential world as real. It regards the world of spirit or of ideas as imaginary—a world of illusions, of nominal inventions. Ideas are merely by-products of the real, material world.

The impact of positivistic thinking on Hegelian philosophy might, one supposes, have had the effect of simply discrediting it and pushing it aside. The prestige of Hegelianism, however, and the appeal of its logical structure, obviated this. Hegel was to the dominant tradition of German philosophy in the first half of the nineteenth century what Aristotle had been to mediaeval philosophy, what Marx would be to philosophy throughout the Communist world. Whatever philosophical views were put forward, however anti-Hegelian they might be, had to be put forward in the name of Hegelianism. They had to be considered as developments or transformations of Hegelianism. Positivistic thinking, therefore, instead of annihilating or displacing Hegelianism, transformed it, keeping the name (with modification, as 'neo-Hegelianism,' 'post-Hegelianism'). The duality of spirit and flesh, of noumenon and phenomenon, of idea and matter, was kept; but the relationship between them, as primary and secondary, was reversed. The material world was given primacy over the world of ideas.

Ludwig Feuerbach is the principal link between Hegel and Marx. His *Essence of Christianity*, published in 1841 (ten years after Hegel's death, the year Marx completed his doctoral dissertation at Jena), caused a stir in the philosophical world of the Hegelians, and completely seduced Marx. As Engels later put it, what Feuerbach maintained was that 'nothing exists outside nature and man, and the higher beings our religious fantasies have created are only the fantastic reflection of our own essence.'[4]

This reversal of Hegelianism, as it appears to be, was presented as being, rather, an interpretation of Hegelianism (an interpretation that transformed it). The device by which this was accomplished is of significance because it would later be used by Marx, and still later something like it would be used by Marxists for the transformational interpretation of Marxism. The device was to make play with a distinction between the *manifest* content of Hegel's philosophy, which anyone could glean for himself by reading Hegel's words, and the *latent* content, which could only be brought out by interpretation. According to the *manifest* content of Hegel's philosophy, God is the ultimate reality of which existential men and things are incomplete aspects. This *manifest* content, however, contains a hidden, esoteric, and recondite revelation. The revelation is that, while existential man and God (*qua* idea) stand in an alienated relation to each other, the reality is not God (as in manifest Hegelianism) but man, God being merely a projected figment of man's imagination. One might say that the *latent* truth in the statement that God created man in his own image is that man has created God in his own image. This is the positivistic mirror-image of the idealist conception.

By inventing religion, Feuerbach said, and by projecting an image of an external God, man alienates himself; he externalizes his noumenal self. 'The real relation of thought to being,' Feuerbach wrote, 'is as follows: "*Being is subject, thought is predicate*. Thought proceeds from being, not being from thought." '[5] Man is being; God, thought.

[4] Engels, *Ludwig Feuerbach and the Outcome of Classical German Philosophy* (1888); English edition, London, 1947, p. 21. 'One must himself have experienced the liberating effect of this book to get an idea of it. Enthusiasm was general; we all became at once Feuerbachians' (*ibid.*, pp. 21–2).

[5] *Kleine Philosophische Schriften* (*1842–1845*), ed. by Max Gustav Lange, Leipzig, 1950. (Quoted by Tucker, *op. cit.*, p. 87.)

This revolution in Hegelianism is one of the foundations of Marxism, with its materialistic emphasis. It also has implications for the meaning of alienation: by attributing all his best and most essential qualities to an external God, man denatures himself, converting himself into an impoverished and essentially alien being. It follows that emancipation from religion is the only escape from alienation.

Marx began by accepting Feuerbach's transformational criticism of Hegel in its entirety. But he did not stop there. He continued the development of that criticism from the point at which Feuerbach left off. Feuerbach had been concerned only with understanding for its own sake (like a practitioner of pure science), while Marx was concerned to understand so as to be able to change (like a practitioner of applied science). Marx was commenting on Feuerbach when he said: 'The philosophers have only *interpreted* the world, in various ways; the point is to *change* it.' If, as Feuerbach and Marx agreed, the illusions of religion were bad, then in Marx's estimation it was necessary to remedy the matter. It was necessary to change the *real* situation that gave rise to the illusions. 'For example,' he wrote, 'after the earthly family is seen to be the secret of the holy family, one must proceed to destroy the former both in theory and practice.'[6] In other words, if God the Father is a projection of the *Herr im Haus*, if the Holy Family of Mary, Joseph, and Jesus is a projection of the family as a social institution among men, then the way to abolish the illusion of a heavenly society is to abolish the earthly society of which it is merely a projection. Marx was a true radical: he tended always to go all the way down to the root of the matter.

Man's alienation, according to Feuerbach, is a function of his religious illusions. More essentially, according to Marx, it is a function of the existential situation of which the illusions

[6] Marx and Engels, *The German Ideology*, New York, 1939, p. 198. (Quoted by Tucker, *op. cit.*, p. 101.)

are merely a symptom. Specifically, man's alienation is a product of the state, which gives man a dual character: as real person and as citizen. 'Only when real individual man,' Marx wrote, 'takes back into himself the abstract citizen of the state and, as individual man, in his empirical life, in his individual labor, in his individual relations, becomes a *species being*; only when man recognizes and organizes his *"forces propres"* as *social* forces and so ceases to separate *social* power from himself in the form of *political* power—only then will human emancipation take place.'[7]

So Marx came to be concerned with what he called 'the unholy forms' of alienation, as well as with the holy. He came to be concerned with 'material' or 'political-economic' alienation. This led him, early in 1844, to take up a study that would absorb him for the rest of his life, the study of economics. It is at this time that a sort of pre-Marxism, an early philosophical version of Marxism, develops, revolving around the idea of human self-alienation in the economic life.

Marx and Engels were both preceded along this line by a somewhat older man. In 1842, Marx, then about twenty-four, was editing the *Rheinische Zeitung* in Cologne. He and Engels, twenty-three years old, were both influenced by Moses Hess, with whom each separately (they hardly

---

[7] Marx and Engels, *Historisch-Kritische Gesamtausgabe. Erste Abteilung*, Vols. I–V, eds. D. Rjazanov & V. Adoratski, Berlin, 1927–32, I/1, p. 599. (Quoted by Tucker, *op. cit.*, p. 105.) The reference to the transformation of the individual into a 'species being' is of interest in its implications of collectivity. Feuerbach had written: 'The being of man is given only in communion, in the unity of man with man, a unity resting on the reality of the distinction between the I and the Thou. . . . Man for himself is man in the ordinary sense; man in communion with man, the unity of the I and Thou, is God.' (From *Kleine Philosophische Schriften, 1842–1845, op. cit.*, p. 169. Quoted by Tucker, p. 91.) In the whole Jacobin tradition, and in Teilhard de Chardin (see footnote on p. 160 below), the individual realizes himself by losing himself in the collectivity.

knew each other at the time) had philosophical discussions. Hess converted Engels to philosophical communism rather quickly, and in time he converted Marx as well.[8]

Hess's thesis was that productive activity is the essential attribute of man. (This is reflected in the illusion of divine creativity, a projection of real human creativity like the projection of the real human family in the holy family.) The life of the species is one of cooperative production, by means of which men translate their productive powers, which are subjective, into a variety of useful material objects external to themselves. Unfortunately, however, the productive power of the species is then seized upon by egotistical men who convert its objectified products into money and private property. Accordingly, Hess said, 'Money is the product of mutually alienated men; *it is externalized* [entäusserte] *man.*'[9]

See what has happened, now, to Hegelianism. Feuerbach held that religion represented the externalization of man's selfhood, and therefore his alienation. Now Hess holds that money represents the externalization of man's selfhood, and therefore his alienation. Hegel's philosophical framework is kept intact, but entirely new categories are hung upon it, replacing the old.

Just as Marx accepted Feuerbach's transformational criticism of Hegel, but kept on going, so he now accepted Hess's transformational criticism of Feuerbach's transformational criticism – but kept on going. Hess's alienated man (alienated by the externalization of his production in the form of money and private property) at last became Marx's proletariat. As Marx's thinking developed, the tragedy of alienation would come to be represented by a social class, the proletariat, which saw its essence alienated by greedy exploiters.

The point now reached has its expression in Marx's *Introduction to the Criticism of the Hegelian Philosophy of Right,*

---

[8] *Cf.* Hess: *Philosophische und sozialistische Schriften, 1837–1850,* Berlin, 1961, pp. xxiv, xxix, xxx, and xlii–xliii.   [9] *Ibid.,* p. 335

written at the end of 1843. Here he refers for the first time to 'the proletariat,' the abstract hero of the mythic vision that is about to come to him. 'The proletariat,' he writes, 'represents the *complete loss of man* and can only regain itself, therefore, by the *complete resurrection of man*.'[10]

The stage has now been set for the great morality play of modern times, 'The Fall and the Resurrection of Man.'

[10] Marx & Engels, *Historisch-Kritische Gesamtausgabe, op. cit.*, pp. 619–20. (Quoted by Tucker, *op. cit.*, p. 114.) The curse of German philosophy is the vague and grandiose language, such as this, in which it is written. Another example: 'Communism,' Marx wrote, 'is the solution of the riddle of history'—to which he added, 'and knows itself to be this solution.' (*Economic & Philosophical Mss.*, in Bottomore, *op. cit.*, p. 155.) How, one may ask, can 'Communism' know anything? Again: 'Private property does not know how to change crude need into *human* need; its *idealism* is *fantasy, caprice* and *fancy*' (*ibid.*, p. 168). This represents the constant tendency of German philosophy to make a corporate entity of every conceptual abstraction, even to make an independent person with an independent will of it. The common vocabulary of German philosophy is a mythical vocabulary. It is an offense against what Marx, himself, would refer to as 'the real, empirical' world.

One of the myths Marx created about himself was that his doctrine had been formed on the basis of *a priori* empirical evidence from the material world. This reflects his concept of matter as preceding mind. (In the Beginning was Flesh, and out of Flesh came the Word.) The vision of *The Communist Manifesto*, however, represented the German intellectual tradition of *a priori* concepts. In this respect he was the opposite of his contemporary, Alexis de Tocqueville, who travelled in America to study a democratic society at first hand, empirically, reserving his conceptual conclusions until he had made himself directly familiar with the facts. The actors in Marx's vision of history were those conceptual abstractions called social classes. He did not derive them from direct knowledge of material men and women. Such knowledge as he had of the proletariat, for example, he got from books. He did not himself come from a working-class background, was not himself a working man, was never associated with working men, and did not find out about the conditions of industrial employment by visiting the factories.

We must be careful, however, to distinguish the young Marx, with his German cast of mind, from the Marx who, beginning in 1849, lived the remainder of his life in London. The English Marx who wrote *Capital*, by contrast with the earlier German Marx of *The Communist Manifesto*, represents the Anglo-Saxon empirical tradition. His original vision of history is still the matrix of his thought, but now he elaborates it on the basis of statistical data derived from existential reality.

With Marx, the idea of empiricism came first, but was realized only in the second half of his career. Then, at last, the Word was made Flesh.

Chapter 5

MARX AND MARXISM

THE nominal is always more real to us than the real. Christ taught poverty and humility, but if an ostentatious and wealthy clergyman bears the name of Christian we do not doubt that he is a follower of the teachings of Christ. Although what Marx prophesied was the self-liberation of the masses, when an adventurer like Stalin emprisons the masses in the name of Marxism, then Marxists and anti-Marxists alike assume that he is fulfilling Marx's prophecy.

The occasion for this observation is the general assumption that Marx had a scientific mind disciplined by empirical reality. In fact, however, what entranced him was not empirical reality itself but the idea of empirical reality. Like Socrates, he inhabited the world of ideas rather than the world of existential phenomena. He was an idealist who made an ideal of empirical reality, and when he denounced idealism in others he was merely denouncing the idealism that makes anything else its ideal.

Rather than a scientist, Marx was an artist. He had the dramatic imagination of a Shakespeare, and since he lived the life of alienation in nineteenth-century Europe his dramatic imagination was more than tinged with romanticism. His first attempts at writing were in the field of poetry. Paul Lafargue, who had been his close associate, wrote of him after his death:

He knew Heine and Goethe by heart and often quoted them in his conversations; he was an assiduous reader of poets in all European languages. Every year he read Aeschylus in the Greek original. He considered him and Shakespeare as the greatest dramatic geniuses humanity ever gave birth to. His respect for Shakespeare was boundless: he made a detailed study of his works and knew even the least important of his characters. His whole family had a real cult for the great

English dramatist; his three daughters knew many of his works by heart.[1]

His daughter, Mrs. Eleanor Marx-Aveling, in her affectionate reminiscences of her childhood, wrote:

... to me, as to my sisters before me, he read the whole of Homer, the whole *Niebelungen Lied*, *Gudrun*, *Don Quixote*, the *Arabian Nights*, etc. As to Shakespeare he was the Bible of our house, seldom out of our hands or mouths. By the time I was six I knew scene upon scene of Shakespeare by heart.[2]

In *Capital* he repeatedly cites passages of Shakespeare (as well as of Greek and Italian classics in the original language), sometimes quoting them at length.

Marx even produced a children's version of the mythic drama that was his life-work. One of the stories that he made up to tell his children, according to Mrs. Marx-Aveling, was of Hans Röckle,

a Hoffmann-like magician, who kept a toyshop, and who was always 'hard up.' His shop was full of the most wonderful things – of wooden men and women, giants and dwarfs, kings and queens, workmen and masters, animals and birds as numerous as Noah got into the Ark, tables and chairs, carriages, boxes of all sorts and sizes. And though he was a magician, Hans could never meet his obligations either to the devil or the butcher, and was therefore – much against the grain – constantly obliged to sell his toys to the devil. These then went through wonderful adventures – always ending in a return to Hans Röckle's shop.[3]

Unless we understand Marx as primarily a man of literary imagination we do not understand him at all. His completed conception of history belongs to the category of dramatic literature, and this accounts for its hold on men's minds.

About the end of 1843, Marx's dramatic imagination began to acquire, as one of its properties, a protagonist called 'the proletariat.' Just as some dramatists had taken the

[1] In Fromm, *op. cit.*, p. 224   [2] *Ibid.*, p. 251   [3] *Ibid.*, p. 251

prostitute to represent the alienated victim of a ruthless and hypocritical bourgeois society, so Marx took the proletariat. He got his idea of the proletariat, however, not from visiting proletarian communities and observing the actual individuals at work and at play, but from books. In the 1840's the proletariat was unknown in his native Germany except through socialist and other writings that described the new class of urban industrial workers in France. There is circumstantial evidence that Marx's concept of the proletariat was largely derived from a report on socialism in France prepared at the order of the Prussian Government by Lorenz von Stein, published in Leipzig in 1842. Von Stein, an anti-revolutionary working for an old-fashioned monarchy, was naturally hostile to this new phenomenon, the urban proletariat. He regarded it as a sort of rabble outside the bounds of polite society and threatening to it. Propertyless itself, it tended to be against the private property of the solid and respectable classes. Undisciplined, it was disposed to be defiant of the law that respectable people upheld. By its sheer mass it was, potentially, a revolutionary force. One can picture Marx falling in love with Von Stein's dangerous monster as one might fall in love with the hero of a novel. Hitherto he had been thinking in abstract terms of 'man as a producer' who suffers alienation in the consequences of his production. This 'man as a producer' was no particular man or group of men. It was what Marx himself called a 'species being.' What Von Stein described, however, represented actual people in the new industrial communities that were growing up in France; and not only actual people but alienated people; and not only alienated people but people who by their increasing numbers and their revolutionary disposition might actually be able to overthrow the societies from which they were alienated. Marx did not himself know them, but only of them. He had the assurance of scientific, empirical studies by Von Stein and others that they existed in real life. Not their empirical reality, but the idea of their empirical reality was what appealed to him.[4]

The empirical individuals did not appear as such to the writers who wrote about social conditions in France, since the human mind cannot encompass, simultaneously, great numbers of persons in their individuality. The abstraction of social class was made surrogate for them; and a class is not an empirical reality, it is an idea. The proletariat, for Marx, was not an empirical reality but an idea that he associated with the idea of empirical reality. It might, one supposes, have been a less crude and simple idea if he had done some empirical research into its basis. In that case, however, it would have been a less satisfactory protagonist in the great morality play that was now taking shape in his mind.

I am anticipating, however, for the role of the proletariat was to shape itself only gradually in Marx's mind between 1843 and 1847.

At the end of 1843, all the elements of philosophical Marxism were already in his mind, but they had not yet been brought together in one coherent plot. Any creative writer knows this moment when something is about to be born within him. There are intimations of the subconscious mind at work, a tendency to detach oneself from one's surroundings, a sense of suspense. It is a time for going on long, solitary walks. . . . And, then, typically, the whole thing is precipitated in the conscious mind like a vision on the Road to Damascus. It had happened to St. Augustine in the

---

[4] There are persons who are active in the cause of saving the sperm whale from its threatened extinction even though they have never seen one and therefore have only the word of others that such a beast exists. (I, myself, have never seen a sperm whale but feel concerned at the decline in its numbers.) One reason why the world of ideas is more real to us than the world of existential reality is that the latter is largely inaccessible. We have to take it largely on faith. I have to take the word of others that there are sperm whales —or even that there is an Australia. My twelve-year-old son has not the least doubt that the moon is a quarter of a million miles distant from the earth, but he confesses that he has not measured the distance himself.

garden at Cassiciacum in August 386. It had happened to Descartes, sitting alone by the stove on November 10, 1619. It had happened to Jean-Jacques Rousseau, walking along the road to Vincennes in July 1749. Something like this appears to have happened, now, to Karl Marx. In the late spring or early summer of 1844 he was struck by a revelation.

What was that revelation?

We have to think again in terms of the distinction between manifest and latent Hegelianism, between the overt meaning and the hidden meaning. To Feuerbach, the hidden meaning lay in the realm of human psychology: Hegelianism was a psychological theory in disguise, cryptically revealing that man alienates himself by projecting the mental image of God as an external being. The revelation that Marx now experienced consisted in the discovery that the hidden meaning of Hegelianism lay in the realm of economics: Hegelianism was an economic theory in disguise.[5]

This was the birth of Marxism – at least in its original, philosophical form.

It was in fulfilment of his vision of what Hegelianism really meant that Marx now wrote those papers known as the *Economic and Philosophic Mss. of 1844.*[6] The theme was still the tragedy of man's alienation and the promise of his salvation. Man, in this vision, is the supreme creative artist who realizes himself in the production of material objects, which then become the concrete, external embodiments of his powers. All these material objects, over the ages, transform the physical world. They gradually substitute a wholly man-made environment for the primeval natural environment. The latent meaning in Hegelianism,

[5] *Cf.* Bottomore, *op. cit.*, p. 203
[6] Marx and Engels deliberately refrained from publishing these Mss. Their first appearance in the original German was in 1932, in the *Historisch-Kritische Gesamtausgabe*, III, *loc. cit.* They have now been published in T. B. Bottomore's English translation, *op. cit.*

the meaning Hegel intended, is that man, rather than God, is the creator of the world.[7]

The practical construction of an *objective world* [Marx wrote in the Mss. of 1844], the *manipulation* of inorganic nature, is the confirmation of man as a conscious species-being. . . . Animals produce only themselves, while man reproduces the whole of nature. . . . [Man] knows how to apply the appropriate standard to the object. Thus man constructs also in accordance with the laws of beauty. . . . This production is his active species-life. By means of it nature appears as *his* work and his reality.[8]

The world of man's production, however, appears alien and hostile to him. This world that he has himself produced is estranged from him and stands against him. It is estranged because of the way the producing activity is carried on, because that activity is carried on in such a fashion as to

---

[7] '. . . the *whole of what is called world history* is nothing but the creation of man by human labour, and the emergence of nature for man. . . .' Nature is 'a human reality' (*Economic & Philosophic Mss.*, Bottomore, *op. cit.*, p. 166).

It was not only at this early stage that Marx regarded man as the creative artist (Hans Röckle). In *Capital* (translation by Samuel Moore and Edward Aveling, Moscow, 1961, Vol. I, pp. 177–8) he writes that, by 'acting on the external world and changing it, [man] at the same time changes his own nature. He develops his slumbering powers and compels them to act in obedience to his sway. We are not now dealing with those primitive instinctive forms of labour that remind us of the mere animal. An immeasurable interval of time separates the state of things in which a man brings his labour-power to market for sale as a commodity, from that state in which human labour was still in its first instinctive stage. We pre-suppose labour in a form that stamps it as exclusively human. A spider conducts operations that resemble those of a weaver, and a bee puts to shame many an architect in the construction of her cells. But what distinguishes the worst architect from the best of bees is this, that the architect raises his structure in imagination before he erects it in reality. At the end of every labour-process, we get a result that already existed in the imagination of the labourer at its commencement.' This, to my mind, is Marx at the pinnacle of his greatness. Here he anticipates modern evolutionary theory (see my Chapter 10). This is the great and authentic vision. If he had not gone on to develop it in terms that foretold the future specifically, and if he had not vulgarized it in other ways, one could hardly question his title to be numbered among the truly great philosophers. The point for him, however, was not to *interpret* the world but to *change* it. This required the kind of vulgarization that *The Communist Manifesto* represents.

[8] Bottomore, *op. cit.*, pp. 127–8

alienate the producer from himself in the very act of producing. Production, instead of being the free, spontaneous activity of the artist giving expression to his genius, is forced labor for another, imposed labor, production carried on in servitude. The productive activity, Marx writes, is experienced 'as activity for another and of another, living as the sacrifice of life, and production of the object as loss of the object to an alien power, an alien man.'[9]

The root of this evil, as in so many other morality plays, is money. It is the greed for gold that corrupts, transforming free, creative self-activity into alienated labor. How well this corresponds to various stereotypes of nineteenth-century romanticism! There is Goethe's Faust, selling his soul to the devil. There is the prostitute who alienates her body for money. There is the painter in his garret whose paintings are taken from him by the wealthy middle-man to be sold to the *nouveau-riche* bourgeois. Finally, it is permissible to speculate on the subjective element. Marx, himself, was the frustrated and suffering artist, 'Hans Röckle.'

The cumulative spiritual enlargement of man's being in the manifest Hegel becomes, in Marx's exposition of Hegel's latent meaning, the obsessive accumulation of capital. Man is a Kantian split personality, at war with himself: the creative artist at war with the greedy beast who exploits him.

The progressive movement of history marked by the alienation of productive force is different in one important respect from that set forth in manifest Hegelianism. Whereas the movement of history in manifest Hegelianism has the effect of progressively overcoming alienation, in Marx's transformation that movement progressively increases alienation. In the manifest Hegel, as man comes to comprehend the objective world by cognition, he becomes progressively less alienated. In Marx's transformation, as he produces under improper conditions he becomes more and more

[9] *Ibid.*, p. 134

alienated. However, in Marx's transformation, which is so much more dramatic than the original, history still comes to the same end. It comes to that end by a catastrophic total revolution that changes everything, man's nature and the circumstances in which he produces alike. It comes to that end by a revolution in which the greedy beast is captured and destroyed, the Kantian alienation being finally overcome forevermore. This revolution is the Marxian equivalent of the Second Coming. Alienation increases until the last scene of all, when it is overcome by revolution. So Paradise is regained.

Paradise is not, however, regained immediately. There is a period of purgatory before a redeemed mankind can come into its inheritance. This is the short transitional period of what, in the Mss. of 1844, Marx called 'crude communism' – equivalent to what he would later call 'the dictatorship of the proletariat.' One reason why Marx and Engels withheld these manuscripts from publication may well have been that in them Marx described this transitional period as one of infinite degradation. At this penultimate stage of man's progress he has to go through an unmitigated vileness and viciousness as the condition precedent to the self-change that will usher in the Paradise of ultimate communism. In this period of crude communism, greed will become universal; the institution of marriage will dissolve and all women will descend into a state of universal prostitution; private property, recaptured from the capitalists, will minister to everyone's gluttony.[10]

Then, however, at a given moment, human nature will change. Then the utopian anarchy of forevermore will at last prevail. Then, says Marx, there will be

positive abolition of *private property*, of *human self-alienation*. . . . [Communism will become] *the definitive* resolution of the antagonism

[10] In *Revelations* 20, the reader will find a similar prediction of the penultimate. Immediately prior to the establishment of the Kingdom of Heaven on Earth, Satan will be loosed from his bonds for a final fling.

between man and nature, and between man and man. It is the true solution of the conflict between existence and essence, between objectification and self-affirmation, between freedom and necessity, between individual and species. It is the solution of the riddle of history and knows itself to be this solution.[11]

Then there will be transcendence of religion, the family, the state, law, morality, science, art, etc. Then men will produce freely, as artists fulfilling themselves in artistic creation. Then they will realize their natural tendency to arrange things 'according to the laws of beauty.'[12] Then the alienation of men's production will be overcome, for greed itself will have been overcome. As Marx puts it: 'all *objects* become for [man] the *objectification of himself.* The objects then confirm and realize his individuality, they are *his own* objects, i.e., man himself becomes the object.'[13] (This, in economic terms, is simply the Hegelian process of assimilating the objective and alien world to one's subjective self.) And so, finally, there will be no ownership, public or private. There will be no property, not even 'national property.' Man and external nature will have become one.

We should have no difficulty in recognizing this mythic drama, for it is the drama of *Genesis*, of the Holy Grail, of Goethe's *Faust*; it is the drama of Odysseus; it is the story of Cinderella. It is the universal myth of mankind, so much so that one wonders whether it must not, in its essence, be

[11] Bottomore, *op. cit.*, p. 155
[12] In *The German Ideology* Marx wrote that 'in the Communist society, where each one does not have a circumscribed sphere of activity but can train himself in any branch he chooses, society by regulating the common production makes it possible for me to do this today and that tomorrow, to hunt in the morning, to fish in the afternoon, to carry on cattle-breeding in the evening, also to criticize the food—just as I please—without becoming either hunter, fisherman, shepherd or critic.' (Selected writings of Marx, edited by Max Eastman, under the short title *Capital*, New York, 1932, p. 1.) In anyone else, this would be identified as utopianism. It is not so identified in Marx when one starts from the premise, based on his own claims, that he was an anti-utopian empirical scientist.
[13] Bottomore, *op. cit.*, p. 161

true. In *Genesis*, God created man in his own image—*i.e.*, made him a divine creature. But man also had an element of greed that moved him to taste of the forbidden fruit, thereby bringing about his fall, his expulsion from Paradise. In Marx's rewriting, man was an artist of divine creativity. But he also had an element of greed which moved him to sell his creations for gold. Just as Adam and Eve found themselves in an alien world as a consequence of their greed, so Marxian man found himself the inhabitant of an alien world that he had brought into being by his greed. In Christian theology, Paradise is finally regained after the Second Coming and the Day of Judgment. In Marx's vision, Paradise is finally regained after the Revolution.

* * *

What I have just described is the original, philosophical Marxism, as set forth in the Mss. of 1844. How does it differ from the mature Marxism of *The Communist Manifesto* (1848), which has its first expression in Marx's *The German Ideology* (1845–6)?

Marx's original protagonist was that great abstraction, man, undivided and undifferentiated, the 'species being.' The conflict of the historic drama was an inner conflict, as it had been ever since Kant. The difficulties this posed, for a dramatist seeking a clear-cut, workmanlike resolution of the conflict, would naturally have moved Marx increasingly to think of the two antagonists within the 'species being' as two persons, as Dr. Jekyll and Mr. Hyde. This tendency, carried to its implicit conclusion, constitutes the difference between the original and the final Marxism.

In the final Marxism man has disappeared. The 'species being' is gone. There is no such thing in the empirical reality to which Marx was always appealing. Man, however, is not replaced by individual men. The real actors in Marx's drama are two social classes: the proletarian and the capitalist. They have now become separate persons, rather than separate aspects of the same person. In *The Communist Manifesto* he and Engels will express their contempt of German socialism because it has espoused, 'not the interests of the proletariat but the interests of human nature, of man in general, who belongs to no class, has no reality, and subsists only in the misty realm of philosophical fantasy.' The proletarian is the good man, the creative artist. The capitalist is the bad man, the embodiment of greed. The great drama of good and evil, of man's fall and his redemption, of Paradise lost and Paradise regained, remains essentially the same. But it is made less abstruse, it is simplified by having different actors represent its different elements. I might have a hard time explaining the drama of split personality to my younger children; but I would have no difficulty at all explaining the drama of the Good Proletarian and the Wicked Capitalist. Hegel, and the transformational criticism of Hegel, had not been for the common mind. The final Marxism was. It had the advantage over the Kantian concept of inner conflict within one person that it represented the fallacy of the two species, which is native to the common mind.

This conversion of the inner conflict into an outer conflict ostensibly (but only ostensibly) eliminated the theme of alienation.[14] Man had been alienated from himself; but the proletarian's alienation takes the form of enslavement, and the term 'alienation' is no longer used. In the revolution, the proletarian will not, ostensibly, overcome alienation, he will overcome the capitalist.

In the final version of Marxism there is a hero called the Proletariat and a villain called the Capitalist. The villain holds the hero in bondage and tortures him. But—the hero

---

[14] 'It is of the utmost importance for the understanding of Marx to see how the concept of alienation was and remained the focal point in the thinking of the young Marx who wrote the *Economic and Philosophical Manuscripts*, and of the "old" Marx who wrote *Capital*' (Fromm, *op. cit.* p. 51).

is growing in his strength all the time, and secretly his wrath is rising even as he continues to stoop under the villain's yoke. So history approaches its last act: the day when the hero shall suddenly rise up, and cast off his yoke, and burst asunder his chains. Then shall the mighty fall. Then shall the cringing villain, the erstwhile persecutor and exploiter, be cast down. Then shall the Capitalist be consumed in the Proletariat's vengeance.

* * *

We understand Marx best as a visionary who was overcome by a great dramatic vision, false or true, on the Road to Damascus. We understand him best as the maker of a myth, for his vision was of an essentially mythic world.

To say this is not to render a judgment on the truth or falsity of Marxism, for myth is one of the forms in which truth is expressed, and in which it is apprehended by us limited mortals. What I regard, for example, as the myth of the Fall of Man in *Genesis* surely expresses a truth—the same truth as takes a different form in the works of Sigmund Freud, who was also a great myth-maker.

Myths may express truth, but they express it symbolically rather than literally. A century of history, by failing to realize any of Marx's fundamental predictions, has shown that, in a literal sense, the Marxian myth was false. But this is to be expected of any myth. The question to ask, therefore, is whether it represents some truth, not literally but symbolically.

'The projection of an inner moral drama upon the outer world is the essence of myth.'[15] The inner moral drama that is the essence of Marxism is the classic drama of man's alienation—the theme of so much literature from the Greek myths, and from *Genesis*, to our own day. The projection upon the outer world of this inner moral drama takes the

[15] Tucker, *op. cit.*, p. 229

form of a contest between the two halves of a mankind that has become divided against itself. What is symbolized is the conflict between the two selves, which is the theme of Kant, Hegel, and Feuerbach, which is Marx's 'manifest' theme until that moment in 1844 or 1845 when it finally is translated into the dramatic myth of good and evil, of the two social classes as contending persons like God and Satan—the whole ending in the eschatological beatitude that follows the ultimate triumph of the good.

*   *   *

Appreciating Marx in these terms, it becomes understandable that he should appear in modern history as a figure of such Titanic power. It becomes understandable that his thought captured the imagination of people all over the earth, that it had the power to sway whole nations as the rantings of a Bakunin or the fabricated myths of an Auguste Comte could never do.

Marx was not a sinister character bent on destroying civilization by devious devices. He was no more a villain on the scene of history than Joan of Arc was. He was, rather, a man of a vast literary imagination, nourished on Aeschylus and Shakespeare, who had a mythic vision that, in the circumstances of the industrial revolution as it had developed by the middle of the nineteenth century, was destined to move men with the power of a new religion. At a time when factories were mushrooming in England and on the Continent, when millions of people were losing their ancient independence and becoming wage-slaves to the owners of the new machines—at such a time, what could have greater appeal than this drama in which the oppressed proletarian, suddenly in the last act, overthrows the capitalist tyrant, bringing into being the Kingdom of Heaven on Earth?

The Gospel story had promised the poor and downtrodden of the Roman world that they should be first, and the first should be last, on the Day of Judgment that was expected within an imminent or, at least, a foreseeable future. This myth had solaced half mankind for nineteen centuries. With industrialization and urbanization, however, it began to seem remote and unreal. Jesus had spoken to shepherds in pastoral terms, not to factory-workers in the terms of an industrial society. Marx's mythic vision, then, filled the growing emptiness of belief, offering to city-workers the hope and the promise of their redemption and salvation—on that day of final judgment when the trumpet should at last blow the signal for revolution. Then 'the first shall be last; and the last shall be first.'

Marxism met the city-man's need for a new body of belief. It met the need for a religion of the industrial age.

Chapter 6

MARXISM AFTER MARX

D R. Heinrich Karl Marx was a man of compelling imagination. He marshaled all history for the composition of his vision, showing how it had been no more than a process of gestation for the new world that now, at last, was about to be born. Since everything was explained in these terms—science and industry, literature and art, religion and philosophy—everything contributed to the conviction which these terms carried. They offered a new intellectual or spiritual haven to men who had been set adrift from their old moorings.

In *The Communist Manifesto*, after summarizing the history of mankind up to the time of its composition, Marx and Engels foretold the future. 'Society as a whole,' they said, 'is more and more splitting up into two great hostile camps, into two great classes directly facing each other—Bourgeoisie and Proletariat.' As the bourgeoisie develops and its capital increases, so the proletariat develops as a class of laborers 'who must sell themselves piecemeal, [who] are a commodity, like every other article of commerce.' As machines develop, the proletarian's work becomes constantly less skilled and therefore less satisfying to him. 'In proportion as the use of machinery and division of labor increases, in the same proportion the burden of toil also increases . . .' and the wage comes to be merely a subsistence wage, representing the means of subsistence that the proletarian requires 'for his maintenance, and for the propagation of his race.' 'The modern laborer . . ., instead of rising with the progress of industry, sinks deeper below the conditions of his own class. He becomes a pauper, and pauperism develops more rapidly than population and wealth.'

As this process continues inexorably, the proletarian

becomes conscious of belonging to a cosmopolitan class of wage-slaves exploited by a cosmopolitan bourgeoisie. This proletarian class is constantly rising in strength and class-consciousness even as it sinks in misery. It 'not only increases in number; it becomes concentrated in greater masses, its strength grows, and it feels that strength more.' As 'entire sections of the ruling classes are, by the advance of industry, precipitated into the proletariat, [they] supply the proletariat with fresh elements of enlightenment and progress.' The ruling class is 'in dissolution.' 'The decisive hour' approaches, 'when the violent overthrow of the bourgeoisie lays the foundation for the sway of the proletariat.'

The prophetic vision that the Manifesto sets forth is clear and simple. As more and more of the total population sinks into the ranks of the proletariat, swelling them, the proletarians themselves sink increasingly to a dead level of mere subsistence. Capital becomes more and more concentrated in the hands of 'industrial millionaires – the leaders of whole industrial armies, the modern bourgeois.' The proletariat, however, becomes class-conscious, organizing its increasing strength even as the weakening bourgeoisie, torn by its own inner conflicts, tends toward dissolution. The revolutionary movement that, at the decisive hour, caps the climax is that 'of the immense majority, in the interest of the immense majority.' When this immense majority bestirs itself, 'the whole superincumbent strata of official society [are] sprung into the air.'

*　　*　　*

I noted at the beginning of the last chapter that the nominal is always more real to us than the real. This is relevant to the single-mindedness with which we cling to predictive visions long after existential circumstances have failed to bear them out.

Jesus, on the Mount of Olives, was asked by his disciples when the Second Coming and the Day of Judgment would occur. 'Truly, I say to you,' he replied, 'this generation will not pass away till all these things take place.'[1] The first generation of Christ's followers based themselves on this prediction, taking no thought for the morrow, discouraging marriage, not bothering with the training of children, not organizing themselves for the perpetuation of the Gospel. The prediction, however, was not borne out. Some came to expect, then, that the year 1000 would bring the ending of the world and the Day of Judgment. This year also passed, yet the imminence of the world's ending continued to be preached by some Christian sects. The immediate predecessors of today's Seventh Day Adventists established October 22, 1844, as the date of the world's ending, a date that Karl Marx would have found premature.

During the years when he was writing *Capital*, Marx was sometimes afraid that he would not get it finished before the proletarian revolution occurred.[2] We now know that he need not have worried.

Marx never drew up a time-table for his predictions. What he predicted was the direction in which history would move. In fact, however, from the moment of the Manifesto it became increasingly clear that history was moving in the opposite direction. This posed a dilemma for all those who were committed, irrevocably, to the realization of the prophecy. The continuing and cumulative divergence of history from what had been prophesied as inevitable at last produced the most terrible moral dilemmas, and some of the greatest moral disasters, of modern history. Those who understand

---

[1] *Matthew*, xxiv. 34

[2] Letter to Engels December 8, 1857, quoted by Tucker, *op. cit.*, p. 225, from Marx and Engels, *Selected Correspondence, 1846–1895*, New York, 1942, p. 225. Marx and Engels had allowed themselves to hope that the Revolution of 1848 was the final proletarian revolution. Disillusioned with its failure, in 1850 Marx foresaw that the proletarian revolution might not come about, now, for another 'fifteen or twenty or fifty years.' (See Marx's statement quoted by Bertram D. Wolfe, *Three Who Made a Revolution*, Boston, 1955, p. 484.)

this properly will feel that, after all the tale of blame has been told, the men who have held power in Moscow since 1917 are still not unworthy of compassion. They have all been prisoners of the prophecy that history betrayed.

The Communist vision was plausible in 1848 as it never would be again. The industrial revolution had, increasingly, drawn masses of people from the countryside, from the cottages and farms, into the new urban industrial centers, where they worked at the machines in the factories. The owners of the machines, the *nouveau-riche* capitalists, held the workers at their mercy, setting the terms of employment to suit themselves. Women and even little children, helpless in their wage-slavery, labored at the machines fifteen hours a day, under conditions comparable to those of galley-slaves, and died or were broken to increase the swollen profits of the factory-owners.[3] The power to remedy these evils lay with the state, but the state was slow to intervene effectively – partly because it was, as Marx said, the instrument of the capitalists, and partly because there was a time-lag between the rapid progress of the industrial revolution and a general appreciation of the new social problems that it brought with it.

[3] In *Capital* Marx was able to cite with authority such instances as the following: 'Children of nine or ten years are dragged from their squalid beds at two, three, or four o'clock in the morning and compelled to work for a bare subsistence until ten, eleven, or twelve at night, their limbs wearing away, their frames dwindling, their faces whitening, and their humanity absolutely sinking into a stone-like torpor, utterly horrible to contemplate . . .' 'William Wood, 9 years old, was 7 years and 10 months when he began to work. . . . He came to work every day in the week at 6 a.m., and left off about 9 p.m.' Such children might earn 3 shillings and sixpence per day. In a deposition, one father stated: 'That boy of mine . . . when he was 7 years old I used to carry him on my back to and fro through the snow, and he used to have 16 hours a day. . . . I have often knelt down to feed him as he stood by the machine, for he could not leave it or stop.' (*Capital*, Vol. I, Chap. X, 'The Working-Day,' Section 3, 'Branches of English Industry without Legal Limits to Exploitation.') During this same period, Andrew Carnegie's United States Steel Corporation at one time showed a profit of $40,000,000 in a single year. (Morison & Commager, *Growth of the American Republic*, New York, 1954, Vol. II, p. 134.)

This situation was in process of dynamic development. As industrialization spread and progressed, ever greater concentrations of industrial workers formed, and their misery became more conspicuous even if it did not become greater. The wealth of society was increasingly concentrated in fewer and fewer hands.

By simple extrapolation it was easy to see, in 1848, what the end of this process must be. As the proletariat became increasingly concentrated and conscious of its misery it could not fail to become increasingly revolutionary. The time would come when the capitalists no longer had the strength to hold the proletariat in bondage. Like Macbeth, however, they would find that they were 'in blood stepp'd in so far, that should [they] wade no more, returning were as tedious as go o'er.'

Extrapolation of present trends is the commonest error of those who foretell the future. What Marx did not see in 1848, or what he did not wish to credit, was that the increasingly intolerable situation of the new industralized civilization had within itself corrective elements of its own, that these corrective elements were coming increasingly into play, and that they would reverse the secular trend that he had extrapolated to its logical conclusion. Even if one accepted the most cynical view of capitalist nature, there was no reason to suppose that the capitalists could not foresee the revolutionary consequences of uncontrolled exploitation that Marx foresaw, or move to forestall them.[4] Already in Marx's day it was apparent that the choice lay between reform from within and revolution. Conscious that this was so, Marx vigorously opposed reform (as have the orthodox Marxists

---

[4] Here the mistake was to expect the enactment of the French Revolution, with its antecedents, all over again. In fact, the French Revolution, so vivid still for Marx's generation, was the normative model. Nothing was more plausible to the imagination of that time than its repetition in all essentials. Like the generals who always prepare for the last war, Marx prepared for the last revolution.

ever since), but he could not prevent it from carrying the day. The reader will appreciate the irony of the fact that the circumstantial accounts, in *Capital*, of the exploitation practiced by factory-owners, and of the ghastly conditions of living and labor in the industrial communities, were drawn from the official reports of Royal Commissions authorized by predominantly bourgeois parliaments whose membership included not a single representative of the proletariat. They were documents of the bourgeois state looking to reform.[5]

[5] In his Preface to the first German edition of *Capital* Marx wrote: 'We should be appalled at the state of things at home, if, as in England, our governments and parliaments appointed periodically commissions of inquiry into economic conditions; if these commissions were armed with the same plenary powers to get at the truth; if it was possible to find for this purpose men as competent, as free from partisanship and respect of persons as are the English factory-inspectors, her medical reporters on public health, her commissioners of inquiry into the exploitation of women and children, into housing and food' (*op. cit.*, p. 9). I have, in the two preceding chapters, betrayed a certain scepticism at the insistence that Marx based his doctrine on scientific method applied to empirical evidence. To me it seems unquestionable that this is not so—if we take the period up to 1848, when the doctrine at last appears full-blown. However, with his removal in 1849 to London, where he devoted himself to scholarship for the rest of his life, the intellectual climate of England, perhaps combined with his own growing maturity, led him to practice empiricism as he never had before. He became more English and less German. His doctrine remained, but he subjected it to the empirical test, with the result that, along with Engels, he became less doctrinaire. In his Preface of 1886 to the English edition of *Capital* (*op. cit.*, p. 6), Engels put forward the case for giving the book a hearing on the grounds that Marx was a man 'whose whole theory is the result of a life-long study of the economic history and condition of England, and whom the study led to the conclusion that, at least in Europe, England is the only country where the inevitable social revolution might be effected entirely by peaceful and legal means.' (Engels was speaking very loosely here, since the 'life-long' study of conditions in England did not begin until after the basic theory of Communism had been formulated and published. Engels observes, immediately after the above passage, that Marx 'certainly never forgot to add that he hardly expected the English ruling classes to submit, without a "pro-slavery rebellion," to this peaceful and legal revolution.' This is either inconsistent or to be read in the vaguest sense.) One suspects that, if they had lived long enough, Marx as well as Engels would have been on the side of the 'Revisionists' and against the 'orthodox' Marxists. In fact, before his death, Marx had already told Paul Lafargue: 'What is certain is that I am not a Marxist' (Bottomore, *op. cit.*, p. xiii, fn.).

The existential world had already begun to diverge from the conceptual world of the Manifesto by the time of its publication. In England as early as 1802 the Morals and Health Act had provided limited safeguards for work in cotton mills. The Cotton Mills Act of 1815 had limited the age at which children might be recruited into factories, and had limited their hours of labor to seventy-two per week. In 1844, another Act of Parliament restricted child-labor in certain factories to six and a half hours per day. In 1847, the so-called Ten Hours Act, limiting the hours of work per day for adults, could hardly be overlooked. The increasing organization of the proletariat, said the Manifesto, 'compels legislative recognition of particular interests of the workers. . . . Thus the ten-hour bill in England was carried.' What the ten-hour bill represented, however, was the alternative to all that the Manifesto prophesied—the alternative that, in historical fact, was the one that would be realized.

At the same time that the state, everywhere, intervened with ever-increasing effectiveness to protect the workers, the workers themselves gained political power. Gradually they achieved equal political status and an equal voice in the affairs of those societies that had once been so completely dominated by the bourgeois capitalists. Beginning with the Reform Bill of 1832 in England, the franchise was extended until universal adult suffrage was achieved in 1928.

From 1848 on, then, the class-struggle in England, which was the ripest of the industrial nations, began to abate. The proletariat, instead of becoming increasingly alienated from the society in which it found itself, became increasingly integrated into it. Instead of becoming more revolutionary it came, increasingly, to feel that it had a stake in the preservation of the system that provided the opportunities for its own self-determination and self-betterment. It came to regard that system as its own system, to be defended against the conspiracies of alienated intellectuals at home and abroad, to be defended against those who, in the name of the proletariat, would overthrow it.

What happened in England happened also in America, where class-consciousness had never developed as in Europe, where what Marxists called the 'proletariat' refused to consider itself such, and where the industrial labor-force became, in fact, a bulwark of anti-Marxist conservatism. Today the Marxian stereotypes have no relevance to American society, where capital may be owned by the workers, who have full political representation, who play their part in managing the affairs of state, who drive to work in their own cars, who send their children to the universities, and who find no careers closed to them by class-barriers.

Since the Manifesto appeared the class-struggle has abated, the distinction between classes has tended to disappear. In one country after another we have seen this secular cycle repeated: industrialization tending initially to the creation of an alienated proletariat, but being overtaken at last by the reforms of a welfare-state in which the workers acquire a vested interest. From the beginning of the Marxist movement, therefore, its followers have faced, in an increasingly acute form, the standard dilemma of all ideological movements based on prophetic writings regarded as infallible. They have faced the divergence between the conceptual world to which they have given their allegiance and the existential world as it manifests itself empirically. They have faced the choice between an orthodoxy that is unrealistic and a realism that is heretical.

*　　　*　　　*

'The meager satisfactions that men are able to extract from realty,' said Freud, 'leave them starving.'

The existential world, as we have seen, is chaos in the absence of a conceptual order applied to it. The conceptual order explains it, makes it intelligible, and also provides a basis for reforming it.

When we devise a conceptual order to explain the existential world of past or present, we may suppose that it is based on a record of actual observation. But a conceptual order that undertakes to explain the future is bound to be *a priori*. It describes existential circumstances before they have come into being, depending for its ultimate vindication either on the operations of some historical necessity or on the tendency of prophecy to be self-fulfilling.[6] The conceptual order set forth in the Manifesto rested its authority on the claim that it represented historical necessity, but neither its authors nor their followers were willing to confide altogether to that necessity. By a paradox that manifests itself repeatedly in political affairs, the inevitability of what is predicted incites people to the most strenuous measures for its realization. Marx, himself, was more interested in arousing men to action than in simply explaining the world to them.

The possibility of giving direction to one's life, sanity itself, depend for each of us on the conceptual order to which we submit ourselves. It is the bark that holds us above the sea of chaos in which we would otherwise drown. This is why people give their allegiance so passionately, so unreservedly, and so irrevocably to the grand doctrinal systems that invite their adherence. Those who, in the upheavals of our time, have been torn from such allegiance—as some Communists

---

[6] Prophecies tend to be self-fulfilling because so much of human action can be based only on prediction. If I can convince enough people that there will be a stock-market crash within a week, then there will be a crash within a week simply because the people I have convinced by my prediction will rush to sell their holdings. If I can convince the governments of the United States and the Soviet Union that a great war between them will break out within a month, then a great war between them will break out within a month simply because each will wish to get in the first blow. If I can convince enough people that a successful proletarian revolution will take place within a year, such a revolution will take place simply because so many of them will wish to be in the vanguard on the winning side.

at the end of the 1930's—have testified that the act of breaking it is like a suicide. Rather, then, than allow themselves
to doubt because existential circumstances contradict the
conceptual system to which they have given themselves, they
resort to the most elaborate, ingenious, and far-fetched
devices of exegesis to bridge the gap. The exegetic bridge,
however, may at last become so tenuous that the quality of
belief, in new generations at least, is impaired.

This problem of sustaining belief in the face of a recalci-
trant existential world was to cause the greatest confusion in
Marxist ranks even while Marx was still alive. Exegesis would
go to such lengths that Marx, himself, would deny that he
was a Marxist, and Engels would comment ironically that the
Russian Marxists in exile 'interpret passages from Marx's
writings and letters in the most contradictory ways, just as if
they were texts from the classics or the New Testament.'[7]

Before the end of the nineteenth century the Second International had already been torn by the dissension between
those 'revisionists' who, like Eduard Bernstein, acknow-
ledged the fact that history was not following the predicted
course, and the 'orthodox' whose allegiance to the conceptual
world was such as to withhold any credit from the existential
world. Through the First World War, groups of 'revisionists'
would be repeatedly splitting off from the 'orthodox' movement. The man who would force them to split off, in order to
keep the 'orthodoxy' that he represented pure, was Vladimir
Ilyich Ulyanov, better known to history as Lenin.[8]

Lenin was a determined conspirator who ended by estab-

[7] Letter to I. A. Hourwich, quoted by Wolfe, *op. cit.*, p. 111.

[8] There are semantic pitfalls here. From the point of view of members of
the Second International and its successor, the Socialist International, they
themselves represent the straight line of descent from Marx and Engels, and
it was Lenin's Bolsheviks, later represented by the Third International, who
split off. The Socialist International is the organization of the 'reformers' who
abandoned violence and revolution as means of realizing the Marxist escha-
tology. Although they profess themselves Marxists and have a reverence for
the name, their doctrines bear no close resemblance to what one finds in the

lishing the foundations of a dictatorship more absolute and more brutal than any previously known even in the dark record of imperial Russia. He was not averse to the ruthless exercise of power, to the infliction of death and suffering. He was not averse to terrorism and crime. Under the circumstances, it takes an effort to recall that he presumably did not begin his career as an ambitious conspirator seeking power for himself at the expense of his fellow men. Anyone who grew up under the increasingly irresponsible tyranny of the czarist regime, seeing his fellow men tortured and capriciously destroyed by the minions of an obsolete aristocracy, might well dedicate himself to a career of conspiracy and revolution from motives that were entirely honorable. If, then, an imperceptible transformation takes place in the course of that career, until the achievement of power for oneself becomes the single, overriding motive, the original motive will not on that account be less worthy of honor. What this represents is the corruption of the world, from which no one entirely escapes.

In 1877 Lenin entered the Law School of the University of Kazan. That same year his older brother, also a student at the University, was hanged with three other students for participating in a plot to assassinate the czar. The rest of the student body was rebelliously disposed, and the police thought it prudent to place the younger Ulyanov, among others, under arrest. He was expelled from the University, his career as a revolutionary inaugurated by the initiative of the police. In time it would transpire that revolution was one career not closed to him.

Manifesto. On the other hand, I have put the label 'orthodox' between quotation marks because, while those who bear it have been nominally more absolute in their adherence to the Marxist scriptures, the infallible predictions of which they claim to be realizing, circumstances have compelled them to interpret those scriptures in a fashion that might have surprised Marx and Engels.

The principal revolutionary movement in Russia, up to 1889, had been a movement for peasant revolution. About 1889, the year when the Second International was founded, the young Russian intellectuals came to be more attracted to the Marxist concept of proletarian revolution. One guesses that they found it easier to idealize the proletariat, which they did not know, than the peasantry, which they did. A dictatorship of the proletariat may have been easier to contemplate than a dictatorship of the peasantry.

The application of Marxism to the situation in Russia, however, was remote. Russia was still back in what Marxists called the feudal stage of history, the stage in which France had been before the French Revolution. The developing bourgeoisie had not yet reached the point at which it was ready to overthrow the aristocracy and establish its own state. Industrialization was just getting under way. Before Russia was ready for the proletarian revolution there would (in principle) have to be the bourgeois revolution and the establishment of the bourgeois state, as had happened in France in the decade after 1789; then increasing industrialization would have to produce a growing and increasingly exploited proletariat; the proletariat would have to become organized, class-conscious, and revolutionary; it would have to grow until it had become 'the immense majority' of the population of Russia—and only then would Russia be ready for the second and final revolution, the proletarian revolution. As late as January 22, 1917, Lenin, at the age of 46, was saying that 'we old men may not live to see the decisive battles of the coming revolution [in Europe].'[9] Throughout most of his career as a revolutionary it did not occur to him that he would be the principal figure in establishing what was, nominally at least, the dictatorship of the proletariat in Russia.

---

[9] In the original German: *'Wir, die Alten, werden vielleicht die entscheidenden Kämpfe dieser kommenden Revolution nicht erleben.'* *Sämtliche Werke,* Vienna/Berlin, 1930, Vol. XIX, pp. 455–6.

The great theoretical question that faced the Russian Social Democrats (as the Russian Marxists called themselves) throughout the years when the proletarian revolution was the dream of a far-off future was what part, if any, to play in the bourgeois revolution that would have to come first. Should they compromise their ideological purity by making common cause with the bourgeoisie? Or should they let the bourgeoisie make its revolution unaided, and then work for its overthrow by means of the proletarian revolution? On this question the Russian Social Democrats split in 1903. The so-called 'Mensheviks' stuck to the letter of the Manifesto: all the stages would have to be gone through until that distant day when there was a proletarian majority to seize power, and the Social Democrats must wait to participate in the exercise of state power until then. Lenin and his 'Bolsheviks' agreed that both revolutions, the bourgeois and the proletarian, would have to be gone through successively, but they thought it would be best for the proletariat to make the bourgeois revolution for the bourgeoisie; and they also thought it best that the Social Democrats should not refrain from helping a bourgeois successor government wield power. In fact, the party of the proletariat should try to dominate the government of the bourgeois state.

This, however, raised what is to this day the key question with respect to the Russian Revolution and the Soviet regime that followed it. The revolution of the proletariat, according to the Manifesto, must be the revolution of the immense majority; the dictatorship of the proletariat must be the dictatorship of the immense majority.[10] 'All previous historical

---

[10] This, I suggest, was pure naïveté in Marx and Engels. A dictatorship can theoretically be exercised on behalf of a majority, but a majority cannot itself exercise a dictatorship. Marx, who was writing something equivalent to poetry, never bothered with this question. In 1900 the French socialist, Charles Peguy, said: 'I should like to know who will actually be the persons who will exercise the dictatorship of the proletariat.' It was a good question. Peguy was killed in the First World War before he had been given an

movements,' said the Manifesto, 'were movements of minorities, or in the interest of minorities. The proletarian movement is the self-conscious, independent movement of the immense majority, in the interest of the immense majority.'

Until he actually seized power in 1917 Lenin maintained the position that, after the first and second Russian revolutions alike, the exercise of power must be democratic, must be representative of a majority enjoying freedom for the expression of its will. Between the two revolutions it would be a bourgeois majority (he regarded the peasants as being essentially bourgeois); after the second, it would be a proletarian majority.

The dilemma was clear. Lenin and his Bolsheviks, although they were none of them proletarians, regarded themselves as the élite group referred to in the second part of the Manifesto, the élite group that acts as the vanguard of the proletariat, that represents the interests of the proletariat, that directs its movement. As such, their duty was to take power, when the time came, in the name of a proletarian majority. But there was no proletarian majority, and there could hardly be anything approaching a proletarian majority within Lenin's lifetime. The Menshevik position, of refusing to take power until the conditions foretold in the Marxist scriptures had been realized, was theoretically unexceptional. Lenin, however, was not the man to refuse power. His entire career was a single-minded quest for personal power – although perhaps it should be added that he had no thought of using that personal power in his own behalf.[11] His problem, then,

---

answer. As history turned out, Lenin might have answered: 'I and my associates.' Stalin might have answered, simply, 'I.'

[11] To say this is in itself paradoxical. Lenin had no intention of using power to enrich himself, and when at last he did achieve the power of the state he used it in a self-abnegating fashion, not exalting himself as Stalin was to do. For most men, however, and surely no less for Lenin, power is an end that in itself satisfies the ego. Lenin, like De Gaulle in a later generation, was incapable of participating for long in any movement except as the leader.

was how to take power as the representative of a majority that did not exist. His solution of this problem, first demonstrated in 1903, has been the basis of the entire Communist movement ever since. I shall call that solution the tactic of nominalism.

The so-called 'Second Congress' of the Russian Social Democratic Party met in the summer of 1903 to agree on a program that would provide a basis of unity. Instead of agreeing, however, it split into two main factions. Lenin, finding himself outvoted, deliberately split it, the split occurring between his minority faction and the opposing majority. By clever maneuvering to exclude votes of the opposition, he managed temporarily to have an apparent majority of two votes out of some forty-five. Immediately he took advantage of this temporary condition to name his faction the 'Majority' (in Russian, 'Bolsheviki') and to name the opposing faction that of the 'Minority' ('Menshiviki'). By what was equivalent to sleight-of-hand, he permanently fastened the name 'Majority' to his minority faction, the name 'Minority' to the opposing majority.

Here is the first breath-taking example of the tactic of nominalism. If theory forbids taking power except in representation of a majority, and if in fact what one represents is only a minority, then the solution is to *call* one's minority the majority. This would be the basic tactic of Lenin's Bolsheviks from 1903 to 1917, when they would seize power in the name of a non-existent proletarian majority. From 1917 to the present day it would continue to be the basic tactic of the Communist Party of the Soviet Union, which would call a personal dictatorship 'the dictatorship of the proletariat,' which would call enslavement 'liberation,' which would identify conquest by the Red Army as the proletarian revolution predicted in the Manifesto, which in certain circumstances (*e.g.*, Hungary in October 1956; West Berlin since 1945) would identify almost an entire population as enemies of the people. The tactic of nominalism was Lenin's invention, which since its first practice in 1903 has had some remarkable successes, as we shall see in the next chapter. 1903 is the inaugural year for what George Orwell, in his satiric novel, *1984*, would call 'Newspeak,' with its slogans, 'War is Peace,' 'Slavery is Freedom,' 'Ignorance is Strength'; with its 'Ministry of Truth' that rewrites history, and its 'Ministry of Love' that directs the secret police with their torture-chambers.

Chapter 7

THE NOMINAL REVOLUTION

THE disparity between the conceptual and existential worlds confronts mankind with a constant dilemma. That dilemma is, however, like the disparity itself, a matter of degree. Those who give their allegiance to a doctrinal system involving prophecy are put to the greatest test, since the prophecies belonging to doctrinal systems, taken literally, have invariably been wide of the mark. The ingenuity of the devout in meeting that test constitutes a large part of the burden of history.

Until his actual seizure of power, Lenin had given his nominal support to the concept of individual freedom and majority rule in the making of the revolution that Marx had foretold and that he, Marx's faithful follower, was preparing. In practice, however, he always took whatever measures would promote the centralization of all authority in himself. One issue over which he split the Social Democratic Party in 1903 was that of whether it should make the revolution and assume power even in the absence of the proletarian majority that it was supposed to lead. He said it should not. A more immediate issue on which he split it, however, was that of whether the Party should be broadly based and democratic in its internal structure, or whether it should be small, exclusive, centralized, and authoritarian; whether the direction of the movement should come from below or above. Here, on an immediate issue of power, as opposed to an issue bearing on a remote contingency, he was against the democratic alternative. Throughout his career he would always insist, in practice, on having the revolution directed from the top and center, and he would always maneuver with remarkable boldness and determination to keep himself in the top-and-center position.

Trotsky and others who, in those days, were opposed to Lenin, saw the danger implicit in this. According to Lenin, the dictatorship of the proletariat must be the dictatorship of 'the immense majority' expressing itself through free, democratic methods; but the proletarian revolution was to be led, and the dictatorship instituted, by a small, authoritarian élite. That élite would, initially, find itself in the seat of government. It would be the government. Trotsky, opposing Lenin on this, warned that 'the organization of the Party will take the place of the Party itself; the Central Committee will take the place of the organization; and finally, the Dictator will take the place of the Central Committee.'[1] Not every man has had such poignant cause to regret the fulfillment of his own prophecy.

All of us men are constantly faced with the dilemma produced by the disparity between the conceptual and existential worlds. Not all men, however, are introspective; and in men of action, men whose overriding concern is with the practical problems of the immediate present, the dilemma need not involve any notable inner conflict. All political leaders, to the extent that they have successfully maintained their leadership, have done whatever existential circumstances required for its maintenance, sacrificing the logic of their conceptual worlds if that was necessary. It was because Trotsky, more purely intellectual than either Lenin or Stalin, found this hard to do, that he came to grief. Marx or Engels might have come to grief in the same fashion. But Lenin, however competent he was as an intellectual dealing with the conceptual world, was always a man of action first. His primary objective was to achieve power.

The overthrow of the czar and an attempt to establish the bourgeois state occurred in March 1917, taking Lenin and his Bolsheviks by surprise. Here, however, was a possible opportunity for them to seize power. Should they now follow

[1] Wolfe, *op. cit.*, p. 293

the Marxist scriptures, which provided that the seizure of power was to take place only when the proletariat constituted the 'immense majority,' and that this 'immense majority' should then seize the power directly by itself, under the guidance of the Communist Party? Or should they disregard the scriptures and go ahead anyway? Lenin was like Napoleon, that strange representative of the French Revolution. He had what Napoleon called 'le courage de l'improviste.' His favorite adage was Napoleon's, 'On s'engage, et puis ... on voit.' 'The seizure of power,' he now declared, 'is the point of the uprising. Its political task will be clarified after the seizure.'[2]

I have just compared Lenin to Napoleon. It would have been even more apt to compare him to Macbeth.

Among all the parties that contended for power through the summer and fall of 1917, the Bolsheviks were one minority faction. The so-called 'October Revolution' that brought them into the saddle at last was not a popular uprising. It was a *coup d'état* by a band of conspirators under authoritarian organization. That *coup d'état* was opposed by the principal organizations of the proletariat, the trade unions. The head of the new government that it established was Lenin.

A generation earlier, in a letter to Vera Zasulich, Engels had written: 'People who boasted that they had made a revolution have always seen the next day that they had no idea what they were doing, that the revolution made did not in the least resemble the one they would have liked to make.'[3] The so-called 'revolution' that Lenin made in 1917 did not in the least resemble what he had anticipated in 1903; it did not in the least resemble that 'self-conscious, independent movement of the immense majority, in the interest of the immense majority,' that Marx and Engels had foretold. It was not the Marxian revolution at all. It was not even a

[2] Wolfe, *op. cit.*, p. 296
[3] Marx & Engels: *Correspondence, 1846–1895*, London, 1934, p. 437

revolution in the sense of a popular uprising, and the men who made it had by now become Marxian only in name.

As Lenin had called his minority faction the majority, so he now called his *coup d'état* the proletarian revolution, and called his government the dictatorship of the proletariat.

Until 1917 Lenin had insisted that the dictatorship of the proletariat had to be organized democratically. Accordingly, a constituent assembly of revolutionary parties met in Moscow in January 1918. Showing itself preponderantly anti-Bolshevik on the day of its opening, it was closed the next day by the Red Army, permanently. From now on, whatever elements in the Russian population opposed the group in power would be called 'counter-revolutionary' and would be considered fit prey for the Red Army or the secret police. A tyranny would eventually be set up more absolute and more ruthless than any ever imposed by the czars. None of the Marxist program would be carried out. None of it could have been carried out, for history, as we have seen, had long ago betrayed all of Marx's prophecies. The temporary state set up by the putative proletariat would never 'wither away.'

* * *

The nominal is always more real to us than the real. A whole generation, to which I belong, was brought up believing that Karl Marx's prophetic insight had already been vindicated to the extent that the uprising of the proletariat and the establishment of its dictatorship had already taken place in Russia. In the aftermath of World War II that uprising and the establishment of that dictatorship would also take place in Poland, East Germany, Czechoslovakia, Hungary, Romania, Yugoslavia, Bulgaria, Albania, and China.[4] The prestige of Marxism as an infallible science

[4] In China the 'Marxist' revolution was indeed a mass movement. It was not, however, a movement of proletarians but of peasants, whom Marx and

that had discovered the key to history brought the intellectuals of the West under its sway. Even today, we find anti-Marxist scholars in the West warning us of the gravity of the Marxist menace by pointing out the extent to which the Marxist prophecy has already been realized. In fact, it has not been realized at all.

To this day, the common supposition, among Marxists and anti-Marxists alike, is that the Soviet government is realizing the provisions of the Manifesto in accordance with the technical elaborations provided by Lenin. It is thought to represent the doctrine of Karl Marx, supplemented by the methods and procedures which Lenin prescribed—*i.e.*, Marxism-Leninism. And, since what Marx represented was an essentially noble concern for the industrial wage-slaves who, in his day, were being so brutally exploited to swell the profits of factory-owners, this has given the Soviet government, from the beginning, a respectability that it could not otherwise have had.[5]

The nominal is always more real to us than the real. In 1956, Mr. Khrushchev, First Secretary of the Communist Party of the Soviet Union, shocked the world by denouncing Joseph Stalin, who had ruled the Soviet Union for a generation, as one who had abandoned and betrayed the ideas of Marx and Lenin. By that time, Mr. Khrushchev was speaking in the name of Marxism-Leninism, so that he had to be believed—as Stalin before him had to be believed when he, himself, speaking in the name of Marxism-Leninism, had

---

Engels, in the Manifesto, had identified with 'small tradespeople' and 'shopkeepers' as belonging to 'the lower strata of the middle class.'

[5] For example, we find the Quain Professor of English in University College, London, a devout Christian who is attached to the ideals of a mediaeval society, accepting Stalin's state as a realization of Sir Thomas More's *Utopia*. In a book first published in 1935 he writes: 'Four hundred and two years before it came into existence, [More] sketched out the pattern of the Communist state. Those eyes which Holbein drew, anxiously but fearlessly peering into the future, had seen far indeed.' (R. W. Chambers, *Thomas More*, London, 1938, p. 395.)

said who represented it and who did not. About 1960, however, the Communist regime in China began to denounce Mr. Khrushchev for himself betraying the ideas of Marx and Lenin, claiming itself to speak in the name of Marxism-Leninism. This provoked a worldwide debate over which regime did represent Marxism-Leninism. It was as well for both regimes that Marx was not available to pass on the question.

*　　*　　*

The disparity between the conceptual and existential worlds constitutes the basic dilemma of mankind. As the disparity is a matter of degree, so is the dilemma. What is notable about Marxism after Marx is the degree of the disparity—and, hence, of the dilemma. The essential conditions for a Communist revolution, as Marx had set them forth, were never realized, since history took a course opposite to what he had predicted for it. His devoted followers, whether in Russia or China, had done what existential circumstances dictated rather than what he had foretold and prescribed. They had, however, pretended that what they were doing was, in fact, what he had foretold and prescribed. They had called minorities majorities; they had called a *coup d'état* a proletarian revolution; they had called the dictatorship of an oligarchy the dictatorship of the proletariat.

Lenin seems to have understood the dilemma, and until close to the end of his career he had not abandoned hope for its honorable resolution. If the movement he led had got off the tracks laid down by Marx, it might still get back on again. The hope was that the Communist seizure of power in Russia would immediately produce the uprising of the proletariat and the establishment of its dictatorship in Germany, as well as in Hungary and elsewhere. If the Russian revolution had merged with a general European revolution, a proletarian majority might then have been available to legitimize it. This, perhaps, is what Lenin had in mind in 1917 when he said: 'The seizure of power is the point of the uprising. Its political task will be clarified after the seizure.' He was gambling on a general revolution beyond Russia's boundaries.[6]

The failure of a *coup d'état* in Russia to set off genuine revolution elsewhere represented the final failure of the Marxism identified with the Manifesto. From that time on, the Russian leaders were caught in their own trap, compelled to make shift as best they could. They were a small minority besieged in the Kremlin.[7] The result was national socialism ('socialism in one country') under the personal dictatorship against which Trotsky had warned in 1903. The new regime found itself in a state of siege. Its response was a total mobilization of Russia's industrial, demographic, and military resources, at whatever cost in suffering and destruction to the Russian people. Its response involved it in an exploitation of the masses more complete and cruel than any that had gone before under feudal or bourgeois government.

The tactic of nominalism, however, was continued. The dictator spoke in the name of the proletariat, as the representative of a liberated people; he made war in the name of peace; he practiced imperialism in the name of anti-imperialism; when the Red Army imposed a police-government on a foreign people it called it a people's government; and when the people opposed that regime they were called enemies of the people.

[6] In August 1918, Lenin said: 'All signs indicate that Austria and Italy are on the eve of revolution.... In more stable and stronger nations like Germany, England, and France ... the same process is coming to a head. The collapse of the capitalist system ... is inevitable. The German imperialists have not been able to suppress the socialist revolution.' (Louis Fischer, *The Life of Lenin* New York, 1964, p. 305.) Five months earlier he had said: '... there is no doubting the truth that if our revolution remained the only one, if no revolution erupted in other countries, our position would be hopeless' (*ibid.*, p. 220).

[7] 'We live as in a besieged fortress,' Lenin wrote on August 20, 1918 (*ibid.*, p. 279).

We shall ourselves misunderstand this history if we attribute it to the wickedness of malevolent men. The men, themselves, were the victims of history's failure to bear out the Communist prophecies. They were caught in their own trap. The real cause of all this spreading and proliferating tragedy—at the center of which they stood and of which they were themselves the victims—was an ideal conceptual model of human society that was too wide of the existential reality.

Marx and the followers of Marx, with the noblest intentions, took his vision too seriously. They were insufficiently sceptical. Meeting their own need of a conceptual order to overcome the aboriginal chaos of the world, they allowed themselves to be seduced too completely by a conceptual model that was too comprehensive and too absolute, that required too unqualified an allegiance on the part of its votaries. With the best of intentions they produced the greatest of evils by committing themselves to an abstract and *a priori* good in disregard of existential reality.

The discrepancy between the two worlds always imposes some strain on our belief in the nominal. Because we live so largely in terms of the nominal, however, its contradiction by existential reality can go to notable lengths without breaking that belief. Even the failure of the world to end on October 22, 1844, did not put an end to the movement which had been based entirely on the prophecy that this was the date on which the world would end: exegesis found a way out, belief was saved.

One cannot doubt that Marx believed in his soaring vision—specifically in his prophecies as set forth in the Manifesto. Lenin, too, believed, persuading himself that the achievement of power in Russia by himself and his followers was an essential step toward the realization of the prophecies. Therefore he did whatever was necessary to achieve that power, even though it could not be done within the terms of the Marxist scriptures. Again, once in power he did what was necessary to maintain himself and his party in power. As head of the Russian government, he found himself doing what was necessary to keep the Russian state going, even though what was necessary violated the precepts and principles of Marxism. When the initial measures for the establishment of a Communist economy threatened disaster, he abandoned them in favor of the traditional ('capitalist') arrangements of his New Economic Policy. He was always willing to get off the ideological pathway temporarily, in response to existential circumstances. Getting off it, however, he was never to get back on again.

Stalin, a man of coarser mind and outlook, was also willing to get off the pathway. The best commentary on his career is contained in what is surely one of the most poignant public documents of the twentieth century, Mr. Khrushchev's address of February 24-5, 1956, to the 20th Congress of the Communist Party of the Soviet Union. He had begun his career, not as a Marxist intellectual, but as an organizer of conspiracy and a terrorist. He would, one supposes, have served the Mafia in Sicily or the Capone gang in Chicago as zealously as he served the Communist movement in Russia. Once the way to personal power opened up before him, he stopped at nothing in pursuit of it; once he had achieved it, he stopped at nothing to maintain and exalt it.[8] He was an old hand at crime. He may, in his early days, have been a

---

[8] The experience of personal power tends to bring out the evil in men and make it predominant. The extreme predominance of evil in a man like Stalin tempts us to demonize him in our thinking, to distinguish him from our common humanity to the advantage of our own self-esteem. If we could see all, however, we would see that the other element which goes to make a human being was not lacking even in him. Soso Iremashvili, who had become his opponent, reported the depth of Stalin's devotion to his first wife, who died while both were still young. At her funeral, pointing to her coffin, he said to Iremashvili: ' "Soso, this creature softened my stony heart. She is dead and with her have died my last warm feelings for all human beings." He placed his right hand over his heart: "It is all so desolate here inside, so unutterably desolate!" ' (Wolfe, *op. cit.*, p. 453.) Similarly, Maxim Gorki reported that Lenin, one evening when he had been listening to Beethoven's piano

police-informer against his fellow Bolsheviks.[9] In the purges of 1937–8 he killed off the great majority of the upper strata of the Communist Party of the Soviet Union. He virtually exterminated the Bolsheviks who had made the Revolution.

Did Stalin believe in Marxism?

What does belief mean for most people—especially for those who are not introspective? I suppose that Stalin at first believed in Marxism as something to be believed in. It gave one an outward respectability, may even have made one feel more respectable inside. Many are Christians for no better reason, abstaining from thought where thought might lead to the questioning of a belief that it would be embarrassing not to hold. (Belief, for most of us, is what we decide not to question.) They believe, perhaps, at superficial levels of the mind, but not at deeper levels which they avoid searching. Many who believe in personal survival after death are stricken with the terror of eternal nothingness when death actually approaches. Certainly Stalin believed in the ideology as an instrument for the conquest and maintenance of power. The corruption of all doctrinaire thought is that it becomes a vested interest, bound up with personal power and security, more than a representation of what is conceived to be true.

Surely there was a steady decay and corruption of belief from 1848 to 1953, the year Stalin died. There was undoubtedly some corruption of belief within Lenin's mind from 1889 to 1924. Belief must already have been cor-

---

sonata called the 'Apassionata,' said: 'I know nothing greater than the "Apassionata".... I always think with pride: what marvelous things human beings can do! But I can't listen to music too often. It affects your nerves, makes you want to say stupid, nice things, and stroke the heads of people who could create such beauty while living in this vile hell. And you mustn't stroke anyone's head—you might get your hand bitten off.' (From *Days with Lenin*, quoted *ibid.*, p. 500.)

[9] See Isaac Don Levine, *Stalin's Great Secret*, New York, 1956. Also George F. Kennan, *Russia and the West under Lenin and Stalin*, Boston, 1961, p. 246.

rupt at the time of its earliest presence in Stalin's mind, and long before the end of his career I suppose it had turned to cynicism. So far from favoring Communist revolutions abroad, for the most part he did not want them to occur. A native Communist revolution beyond the area dominated by the Red Army would be out of his control.[10] He no longer believed in world revolution, in proletarian rule, in an eventual withering away of the state, in a transformation of human nature that would make the function of the police obsolete. The Marxist ideology was simply an instrument by which he made himself supreme, a device of propaganda.

And, after Stalin, did Khruschev believe?

Again, I suppose that he believed in Marxism as something to be believed in. It was the abstract norm on which all enlightened minds should be formed. It was the nominal symbol for virtue. It represented the virtue that Stalin transgressed when he put himself ahead of the Party and when he resorted to permanent terror against its members. But I would doubt that Khrushchev, in his own mind, related its specific provisions to any practical possibilities of the existential world. I would suppose that he regarded the belief in an historically imminent Communist conquest of the world as dangerous nonsense. I would suppose that he regarded much of Marxist doctrine as educated Christians regard the first chapter of *Genesis*. I would suppose that, like all the rest of us, he had different levels in his mind, and that there was a lack of consistency among them. I would suppose that there was, in him, a limit to the introspective disposition that leads to the questioning of belief.

In any case, during the dozen years after Stalin's death Khrushchev's policy tended, often by the boldest improvisation, toward the undoing of the evils brought upon the world by those who accepted Marx's vision in preference to existential reality. His policy was directed

---

[10] Kennan, *op. cit.*, Chapter 17, especially p. 253

toward escaping from the trap. It was directed toward stabilizing the international situation, diminishing the severities of the authoritarian system that he inherited, mitigating the sufferings of the populations under Communist rule, enlarging their freedom, and restoring a measure of that human dignity to which he referred in terms that had the ring of sincerity.[11]

Although we do not clearly see, yet, the same corruption of belief in China, we may be sure that it has already gone far, and that it will soon become increasingly apparent. The last strongholds of ideological purity will be the Communist parties of non-Communist countries, where the experience of power and responsibility has not tested the relevance of doctrine, where naïveté may therefore survive unchecked, and where the old sense of alienation from one's immediate environment works in favor of Marxism rather than against it.

This brings me back to the general public belief in the validity of the claims made by those who speak in the name of Marxism. If Stalin had grown cynical about those claims, and if Khrushchev acquired a degree of sophistication about them, the world at large has continued to accept them. Many of our most highly trained experts, perhaps because ideology is their specialty, continue to assert that the great international contest of our day is an ideological struggle in which the opposition represents the ideology of

---

[11] Dealing, in his address of February 1956, with the 'confessions' on which so many court-convictions under Stalin were based, he said: 'How is it possible that a person confesses to crimes which he has not committed? Only in one way—through the application of physical methods of "pressuring" him, of torture, of bringing him to a state of unconsciousness, of depriving him of his judgment, of taking away his human dignity.' The reason why, a few pages back, I called this address 'one of the most poignant public documents of the twentieth century' is that it is clearly the expression of a personal feeling so deep as to transcend even the political purposes that prompted its delivery. It is a profoundly human document, bearing out Mr. Bertram Wolfe's aphorism that, 'as soon as the screws are loosened, men tend to spring back into human shape.'

the Manifesto as we represent that of the *Declaration of Independence*. It is Marx against Jefferson.

Not only simple people, ignorant and credulous, are vulnerable to the kind of nominalism that represented the Bolshevik seizure of power as the proletarian revolution, that represented first the government of Lenin and then that of Stalin as the dictatorship of the proletariat foretold by Marx. Those whom we identify as 'intellectuals' are peculiarly vulnerable. They belong to the Socratic tradition that attaches all value to the world of *a priori* ideas, of abstractions.[12] Their concern is with labels; it is with what a man 'stands for'; it is with how he aligns himself in the nominal world—whether he is a 'fascist' or a 'Communist,' an 'existentialist' or a follower of 'Zen,' a 'Dadaist' or a 'Surréalist'; it is with what nominal school of thought he belongs to—for it is assumed that everyone belongs to a school. These people organize to take common positions; they draft resolutions; they combat doctrinal error. Sensitive to fashions in the nominal world, they are more preoccupied with what is correct than with what is true. Because they live so exclusively in the nominal world, they are of all people the most vulnerable to the tactic of nominalism.

Until the end of World War II nominal Marxism had the kind of special appeal for them that Christianity had had for the poor of Rome. It enabled them to make a virtue of alienation by regarding themselves as an enlightened élite standing in opposition to the unenlightened commercial society of the majority. It told them that they, alone, possessed the science that unlocks history, and that they would have the posts of command in the society of the future. They mastered the special jargon of Marxism-Leninism by which

---

[12] In Plato's *Phaedo*, Socrates asks, 'Is not thought best when the mind is gathered into itself, when it becomes as free as possible of all bodily sense?' He tells Cebes how, in his youth, 'I was afraid that my soul might be blinded altogether if I looked at things with my eyes or tried to apprehend them by the help of the senses.'

they could identify themselves as insiders, by which they could distinguish themselves from the outsiders. Marxism gave meaning and direction and hope to their lives. Above all, it gave them status.

If Marxism was the creed of the fashionably alienated in the 1930's, fascism was the creed of their opponents, of the anti-intellectuals, of those whose program it was to complete the alienation of the semi-alienated minorities by eliminating them completely. Communism and anti-fascism were inseparable in the minds of the intellectuals. Therefore, when Stalin, in 1939, entered into a non-aggression pact with Hitler, and when the two of them proceeded to the joint partition of Poland, their position, already shaken by Stalin's purges of the venerated old Bolsheviks, became ideologically intolerable. This was almost as bad for them as the failure of the world to end on October 22, 1844, had been for the Adventists. International Communism survived it, just as the Adventist movement survived, but it lost the fashionable Western intellectuals, who now all turned around and swam the other way.[13]

Still, however, the intellectuals continued to credit the nominal. Although the international behavior of the Soviet Union was essentially the behavior of Russia under the czars, they accepted at its face-value the claim that its motives were ideological, its purpose to make Marxism-Leninism prevail in the world. Being now opposed to the ideology, they became alarmed at the possibility that the rest of us might not see the danger clearly enough. For example: since the nominal situation was one of unshakable solidarity among all Communist regimes, they insisted that it was wishful thinking to suppose that the Soviet Union and China could ever

[13] There was an interval of confusion and delay, consequent upon the fact that Moscow became our wartime ally against Hitler. My impression is that the chief signal for the pro-Communist intellectuals finally to turn around was given by George Orwell's publication, in 1945, of his *Animal Farm*.

fall apart; and when undeniable evidence began to transpire of differences between them (that had existed from the beginning), they warned that the differences represented only a family quarrel. In short, they continued to credit the ideological claims of the Communists after they had become anti-Communist as they had before. The nominal continued more real than the real.

*   *   *

If I carried the matter no further I should leave a false impression. Up to this point, in these chapters on Marxism, I have referred to the existential world as real, the conceptual as false. This has been the more plausible because the discrepancy between Marx's prophecy and what actually happened has been so wide. But the conceptual is the model on which men strive to shape the existential; and so it acquires a secondary reality of its own. The conceptual exists as a prime factor in the existential situation.

The example I have already given is of the discrepancy between the assertion, in the *Declaration of Independence*, that all men are created equal, and the institution of Negro slavery. In time, the existential was brought increasingly to conform – by the abolition of slavery, and by all that has since been done to realize in practice the equality in principle of the American Negroes.

The so-called 'Russian Revolution' was not, as we have seen, the revolution foretold by Marx; and the subsequent Russian regime has not in fact been what Marx foretold. The Marxian way has not been followed at all. But the myth has remained as a prime force in men's minds. The same intellectual class, preoccupied with the nominal to the exclusion of the existential, is found in Moscow and Leningrad as in New York and London. In fact, the tradition of deductive thinking, native to the Continent and predominant in Marxism, gives that class a larger role in Moscow and Leningrad than in the cities of England and America. The Russian leaders find themselves in the same position as the State Department officials of our earlier chapters, poignantly aware of the demands of the existential world because they are at grips with them; while the Moscow and Leningrad intellectuals, like the utopian professors, can disregard them. The influence of the Marxist ideals, however, is pervasive, and the process of mediation between the two worlds goes on. The Russian political leaders are the prime mediators.

The idealistic side of Marxism—which was, after all, an ideal of human freedom and dignity—has manifested its influence in the revulsion against Stalin's barbarities, and in Khrushchev's efforts to democratize the Russian society. The constant pressure to get back on the rails, from which the movement has strayed so far, continues.

On the other hand, the role of violence in the conceptual world of Marx, and of Lenin after him, has made it more difficult for the Soviet government to avoid the military clashes that, in today's world, imply total disaster. Here we found Khrushchev trying to modify the conceptual world, eliminating the dogma of the inevitability of war, advancing the ideal of 'peaceful coexistence.'

Finally, the fundamental concept of world revolution puts the Russian leaders under the greatest pressure to pursue a policy aiming directly at the violent overthrow of non-Communist regimes.

So we see the constant interaction of the two worlds. The existential world is continuously modified by the requirements of the conceptual, and the conceptual by the requirements of the existential. Both are in continuous flux, both change, until at last each has changed beyond recognition. In the course of this dialectical process of evolution the problems of any particular present are not solved, they simply disappear.

PART THREE

Which examines the evolutionary process by which man creates himself, his dual world being driven forward by reciprocal action between the conceptual and the existential; and which suggests the consequent direction that the society of man is taking.

Chapter 8

MAN ON HIS OWN

Every species, with one exception, has a conceptual model to which it conforms, a model for its physical shape and its behavior alike. The close conformity of the individual members to this model makes it easy for a human observer of any species to give an account of its form, its behavior, and what the zoologists call its life-history. The American golden plover (*Pluvialis dominica dominica*), for example, measures close to 27 cm. from tip of bill to tip of tail; in its breeding plumage it is black below and golden brown above, with a white band running along each side from above the bill to beneath the tail; its bill, its feet, its wings, its tail are each an established length. Every individual of the species conforms so closely to this norm as to be practically indistinguishable from any other.

The model is equally fixed for the plover's life-history and behavior. In early June it arrives at its breeding grounds on the shores of the Arctic Ocean, where it makes a nest of a certain size and shape; the four eggs that it then lays hatch out in 27 or 28 days; its young are on the wing a month later. In August it leaves its breeding grounds and flies across the continent to Labrador, where it fattens itself on crowberries (*Empestrum*) before flying on by way of the Antilles to its wintering grounds on the pampas of South America. In March it sets off from the pampas on its return journey to Alaska, this time by way of Panamá. One could go on to set forth the various sounds it makes and the respective occasions on which it makes them, the motions it goes through in courtship or in combat, its care of the young, etc.

While individual plovers vary somewhat from this norm, the fact is that there is an established scenario for the species that leaves no doubt about the conduct and the way of life proper to it. That conduct and that way of life, moreover, have not changed in essentials over the past ten thousand years.[1]

What applies to the golden plover applies to every other species, with one exception. There is no such model for man (*Homo sapiens*), either in his form or behavior, as exists ready-made for other species. Anyone undertaking to describe man would be at a loss to say how tall he is, what is the shape of his nose, what the color of his skin; for some men are under five feet tall at maturity and others are over six; some have flat noses and some aquiline; some have dark skins, some light. I have seen thousands of golden plovers massed on the pampas of Argentina, all appearing identical; and I have also seen thousands of human beings massed in the Plaza de Mayo in Buenos Aires, no two alike. The contrast between the uniformity of the one species and the variety of the other is not merely a subjective impression: it is statistically verifiable. In the language of the biologists, man is polytypic as other species are not.

Just as there is no one model for man's physical conformation, so there is no established scenario for him to act out. Anyone would be at a loss to say what his courtship behavior was: for it is one thing among the Eskimos, another among the Hottentots, another among the Arabs; it is one thing among upper-class Londoners, another among Londoners of the working class; it was one thing in eighteenth-century England and is another in England today. The wandering albatross (*Diomedea exulans*) has, for tens of thousands of

[1] We do not ordinarily attribute the capacity for concepts to birds. However, a bird raised in captivity, which has never seen an example of the nest proper to its kind, will proceed to build such a nest when its season comes. Somehow it has in its psyche the conceptual model for it. In many species of passerine birds the young of the year leave the nesting grounds ahead of the adults, flying south over the established migration-routes of their species, apparently following those routes on the basis of inherited knowledge. Without self-consciousness, they must still have, in their psyches, a model of what it is proper for them to do.

years, built a nest 45 cm. across, 12–15 cm. deep. By contrast, look at the variety of human architecture. One could describe the social organization of the honey bee (*Apis mellifera*) and the architecture of its hive in terms of norms universally applicable, but one could do nothing similar for man.

We have seen that, without a conceptual order, the existential world is simply the void that was in the beginning, the Chaos that preceded the Creation. The Creation itself, we may suppose, was the act of conception. It must have been, in the first instance, the creation of the conceptual world that is the matrix for the existential.

All species are alike in requiring conceptual models for their imitation, matrices on which to form themselves. Each must have a scenario for its existential representatives to act out, a scenario on the basis of which they are able to make the successive choices that confront them. In the case of the plover, the albatross, and the honeybee, such a model or scenario is supplied ready-made. In the unique case of man, only the rudiments of such a model are supplied ready-made.[2] Man, then, has to make his own model, his own scenario. This is the plight of our kind, this is the challenge it faces. 'The foxes have holes, and the birds of the air have nests; but the son of man hath not where to lay his head.'

For man at the present stage of his development, then, the evolution of the conceptual world depends on his own creativity. He is himself the creator.[3]

---

[2] I refer here to a pattern of instinctive behavior that is most prominent in infants and is of little manifest use to the adult in dealing with environments of unique complexity. When the newly born infant fastens onto its mother's breast and sucks in the milk it is acting out a scenario just as the yearling bird is when it flies over a migration-route that it has not itself experienced or been taught to know.

[3] This, be it noted, is related to the Marxist view referred to in Chapter 5 (see p. 86 above, fn.[7]). It is also the view of the French existentialists represented by Jean-Paul Sartre. It is at least close to the view set forth by Pierre Teilhard de Chardin in *Le Phénomène humain* and by Sir Julian Huxley in *The Uniqueness of Man*.

We men, finding ourselves without a ready-made model for our physical conformation, our behavior, and the conduct of our social relations, are engaged in the enterprise of ourselves creating our own model. This, after all, is what political philosophy is about, and what ideology is about. Thomas Hobbes had one model for the organization of human society, John Locke another; Rousseau, Marx, and Nietzsche had still others. Today, Americans, Russians, Chinese, South Africans, Australian aborigines, and others do not agree on the proper model for man's behavior and social organization. This creates problems of which the honey bees, with their one accepted model for all times and places, have no experience. When the bees swarm, in their season, to found a new hive, there is never any question about what the constitution of the new hive shall be. There is never any question of what role shall be played by the queen, what role by the workers, what role by the drones. All this was long ago established for the species, and so were the respective models for all other species except man.

The problem of the two worlds, of the discrepancy between them, does not exist only for man. It exists for all species. Malnutrition may produce, among the golden plovers, an individual that falls short in its dimensions of the ideal model, and so the discrepancy manifests itself. An adverse wind may drive an individual off the established course from Labrador to South America, bringing it up on the coast of Africa, and so the role of accident manifests itself. Sometimes only three eggs are laid, instead of four. A marauding gull may eat a plover's eggs and destroy its nest. A catastrophe may end a plover's life before it has completed the enactment of its life-history—as if an actor should fall dead on the stage in the middle of *Hamlet*. Every plover, like every man, is suspended between chaos and an ideal order. In the case of the plover, however, not only is the order given, but it is relevant to the possibilities and limitations of its existential world. Although there are individual failures to live up to it, the order can be realized and constantly is being realized within limits of tolerance that are unimportant in their narrowness.

Having to make our own ideal model, we men are likely to discover that any particular model we make does not conform closely to the possibilities and limitations of the existential world. Then, perhaps after agonizing experience and great moral disasters, we have to revise and reform and remake it. This is, essentially, the dialectical process of historical evolution: there is the initial concept, there is the contradiction between it and existential reality, and there is the approach to a resolution by means of modifications in concept and existential reality alike. Any society, following this process, tends to move toward stability—at least to the extent that it is self-contained. For example, the American society, founded on the conceptual order set forth in the *Declaration of Independence* and the Constitution, went through a succession of upheavals (the Civil War being only the greatest) caused by the contradictions between concept and existential circumstances; both the conceptual order and the circumstances underwent modification in the course of those upheavals; they tended to adjust themselves to each other; and the trend was toward increasing stability.

Having to make our own conceptual model, however, we men cannot agree on what it should be. In some parts of the world girls are considered adult and ready for marriage at thirteen; in others they have to be nineteen. (Golden plovers, anywhere and everywhere, are ready for breeding at one year old; wandering albatrosses at three.) In some parts of the world monogamy is the rule, in others polygamy. In Sparta the young were brought up by the state; in Athens by their respective families. The social organization or life-history of no other species shows any similar lack of agreement.

Thomas Jefferson represented one model of propriety for man's social organization, Karl Marx another. The attempt to apply Jefferson's model in America failed in important respects: *e.g.*, Jefferson, not appreciating the industrial revolution and its consequences, had conceived a rural society of land-owners, but his conception turned out to be at odds with the industrialization and urbanization that actually were taking place. Both the model and the existential circumstances were changed in the attempt to match them, however, and so the contradictions between them were progressively reduced. The attempt to apply Marx's model failed catastrophically in Russia, but the same process of change in concept and existential circumstances alike is today tending, nevertheless, to reduce the contradictions between them.

If the dialectical process goes on continuously within societies like those of the United States and the Soviet Union, it also goes on among them. Each, committed to its own conceptual system as the equivalent in human terms of the natural propriety that the hive represents for the bees, opposes rival conceptual systems, trying to discredit them and bring them to grief. On the global scale, then, the contradictions and clashes are greater because there is less agreement on concepts of propriety. More scope remains for chaos. Disastrous collisions, time and again, set back half mankind. But here, too, the process, over the long run, tends toward the reduction of chaos, the resolution of contradictions, and the achievement of increasing stability.

Because we men depend so entirely on the makeshift models to which we severally commit ourselves, we are impelled to attach the value of eternity to them. An Aristotle does not say that the city-state is merely a provisional organization of human society produced in the dialectical process of its development, an arrangement that will give way to others as that process continues. He regards it, rather, as representing for men the eternal propriety that the hive represents for bees. Similarly, a Thomas Aquinas regards the universal mediaeval empire as established by nature; a Mazzini regards the nation-state as so established.[4]

Living as we do, today, in a conceptual world of nation-states, we regard that world as an eternal norm. This falsifies our view of the past and blinds us to the future—as I shall attempt to show in the chapters that follow.

[4] 'Bad governments have disfigured the design of God, which you may see clearly marked out, as far, at least, as regards Europe, by the courses of the great rivers, by the lines of the lofty mountains, and by other geographical conditions; they have disfigured it . . . so much that today there is perhaps no nation except England and France whose confines correspond to this design' (Mazzini, *The Duties of Man and other Essays*, translated by Ella Noyes, London/Toronto, 1907, p. 52).

Chapter 9

THE PRESENT AS ETERNITY

FOR reasons of our own psychological security, we identify the conceptual world to which we are brought up as a universal and eternal norm, we assume that it is the essential matrix of all creation. To the extent that we hear of manifest discrepancies from it they seem to us bizarre. Two crude instances from personal experience may serve to illustrate this.

One concerns a man of limited education but inquiring mind who once told me that he often wondered how people could ever have believed, as he understood they once had, that the Earth was flat. The only response I could think of was to ask him how it was possible for him to believe that the Earth was round. He thought I was being frivolous, since to him the Earth's roundness was self-evident.

The other instance was on an occasion, in the English town of Lincoln, when I left a motorcycle parked for the night opposite the inn where I was staying, in a row of parked cars. About midnight I was sent for by a policeman who was standing, flashlight in hand, by my lone motorcycle in the dark and otherwise deserted street, his whole body charged with indignation. It transpired that all vehicles were supposed to be off the streets by eleven o'clock, when the street-lights were turned out. There was no convincing him that, being a foreigner, I had not known of the rule. 'But,' he kept repeating, 'it only stands to reason!' What only stood to reason was that vehicles must not be left out on the street in the total darkness after lights-out at eleven. He would not believe me when I told him that, where I lived, street-lights were kept on all night. It simply did not stand to reason. It only stood to reason, he said, that lights had to go out at eleven—whether in Lincoln, in America, or on the Continent.

If my Lincoln policeman had become convinced that the customs of his home town were not universal and eternal, his conceptual world would surely have begun to crumble, however slightly, and he would have felt, however distantly, the threat of chaos to his sanity. Like all of us, scholars no less than policemen, he had a vested interest in his parochialism.

Men once thought of the *polis* or city-state as my Lincoln policeman thought of the rule that lights go out at eleven. '. . . it is evident,' wrote Aristotle, 'that the *polis* belongs to the class of things that exist by nature, and that man is by nature an animal intended to live in a *polis*.'[1]

Since the middle of the nineteenth century we have lived in a world in which the nation-state is the norm. We have supposed that it was a matter of natural propriety for every man in the world to belong to one nation-state or another. Colonialism, for example, has been seen as a violation of this natural propriety, depriving colonial subjects of the right of self-determination—*i.e.*, the right to their own national states. Looking at a society like that of China in the nineteenth century, which had been formed on the model of a universal empire like Rome, we supposed that it must be simply another nation-state, and by cultural as well as physical imperialism it was brought to conform. Invaded and dominated by the West, it had to learn to act out a new script, it had to learn to behave like a nation-state.

Regarding the nation-state as the eternal norm for humanity, our disposition has been to assume, not only that it will persist indefinitely, but that something like it has always been. We project the normative concept of our present upon a past that knew it not.

I was brought up and my children today are being brought up on the tales of Charlemagne and his paladins, Roland and Oliver. The historical fact appears to be that, in the year 778,

---

[1] Quoted from Aristotle's *Politics* by Robert Gilpin in *American Scientists and Nuclear Weapons Policy*, Princeton, 1962, p. 3. *Cf.* Chap. II of *Politics*.

many centuries before any of the European nations began to emerge from the chaos that followed the fall of Rome, the great germanic chieftain known to us as 'Charlemagne' (to Germans as 'Karl der Grosse') invaded the Iberian peninsula and laid siege to what is now Saragossa, then a city of the Saracens. A call to march against the Saxons, however, caused him to abandon the siege and retire across the Pyrenees. In one of the defiles of the Pyrenees, the Pass of Roncevaux, a part of his rear-guard was ambushed and destroyed by local Basque tribes. Among those killed in the action was Charlemagne's prefect of the Breton March, Hruodland ('Roland' in modern spelling, or 'Orlando'). From this episode came the moving legend that we all know. Charlemagne, defending France, drove the Saracens back to Saragossa. Returning, then, across the Pyrenees, the rear-guard of the French Army, under Roland, was trapped by a host of Saracens far outnumbering it, and was slaughtered to the last man. The last man was Roland who, as he lay dying, wound his wonderful horn so that the faint sound reached the French host far away, already back in the father-land, and was heard by Charlemagne and Oliver, who turned and rode back too late.

I cite this tale because it is the tale of one of those national defeats (like that of the British at Dunkirk in our own time) that stir national pride. According to it, Roland was avenged by the French Army, which returned to pursue and chastise the enemies of France. The French Army, nominally, is the same Army as the one that fought the Battle of the Marne and saved Paris in 1914.

In point of fact, it would be another seven centuries before even the outlines of a French state began to appear on the map of Europe; and the French state that began to emerge in the fifteenth century would still not be a national state, for there would still not be a French people, a French nation. It would, rather, be a feudal holding, the dynastic possession of the Capetian lords of Paris, having nothing to do with nationality. Joan of Arc was not taking the side of the French nation against England so much as she was taking the side of the Capetians against the Plantagenets, who had, at least traditionally, been as French as anyone else. To our minds, however, projecting the present upon the past, it only stands to reason that the French people, in the fifteenth century, should have resented the presence of the English on their soil.

The concept of the one centralized and universal empire, represented by Rome, survived the collapse of Rome. During the six or eight centuries of chaos that ensued in Europe, the universal empire still represented the norm in men's minds. There had been an existential breakdown, but everyone assumed that there must be a return to the normal order of things. Consequently, as soon as Charlemagne had succeeded in establishing his sway over a wide enough area he had himself crowned Roman Emperor. The order he had established, however, immediately broke down again. Out of the ensuing chaos the feudal system emerged as a new conceptual order, retaining elements of the universal empire in the roles of the Holy Roman Emperor and the Pope.[2]

In its organizational features feudal society was a hierarchy, with emperor or pope at the top, with serfs at the bottom, and with intermediate orders that were categorized with some precision. Every man born to this conceptual model, in its most complete development, was born to a clearly defined role that it was his lifelong business to act out. The man who had, for example, been born a serf was attached for life to the land on which he had been born, the scenario not allowing him to leave it. He had to conform to prescribed rituals; he had to act out prescribed allegiances. And so it was with the esquire, with the knight, with the

---

[2] The conceptual order of the universal empire persists and has its expression today in the institution of the papacy. Nominally, the Roman Empire lasted until Napoleon abolished the 'Holy Roman Empire' in 1806.

baron, with the king, with the emperor, and with the pope. Each had a role to which he was obliged to conform. Perhaps a man could enter a monastery and play the monk instead of the knight, but such choices were strictly limited.

The feudal model was never completed. It was never finally settled, for example, whether emperor or pope stood at the apex of the social pyramid—or, if both stood there together, what relationship the role of each had to that of the other. And by the end of the fifteenth century this never-completed feudal model was already half obsolete.

Changes in the existential environment were contributing to its obsolescence. The development of the long bow, demonstrated at Crécy in 1346, had made the military role of the knight on horseback impossible. The development of artillery had made the continued independence of the feudal baron, behind his castle walls, impossible; and it had destroyed the independence of the walled city as well. The very success of the feudal system in bringing order out of chaos over a wide area had led to an expansion of commerce, the growth of towns, and the development of a new middle class for which there was no proper place in the feudal system.

So we see the development of a new conceptual model from the fifteenth century on. In this new model society is organized into dynastic states, each under an absolute monarch who rules by divine right. The ancient feudal hierarchy now develops, within the framework of the dynastic state, into a stratified system of social classes: the nobility, the rising bourgeoisie, and the peasantry. All authority, in this new model, is concentrated in the king, who exercises it through the agency of the nobility, while the mass of the people is politically inert and obedient.[3]

[3] For the classic literary renditions of the model of the dynastic state see Jean Bodin's *Les six livres de la République* (1576), James I's *The True Law of Free Monarchies* (1598) and *Basilikon Doron* (1599), and Bishop Bossuet's *Politique tirée de l'Ecriture Sainte* (1679, with later additions).

By the end of the eighteenth century, however, this new conceptual model had, in its turn, become increasingly obsolete. The development of cities and the intellectual life of cities; the growing wealth and power of the middle classes; the increasing role of the printed word, and the increasing audience for the printed word; the ascendency of religious tolerance after the Wars of Religion; the development of science and of scientific thinking; the increasing role of the common foot-soldier in warfare, as a corollary of progress in musketry; the increasing democratization of warfare that followed from this; the decadence of an aristocracy that no longer had a useful role to perform—all these developments were leading to a situation in which the king and the nobles were exercising an authority that was losing its legitimacy, a situation in which they were less and less able to govern effectively. They were leading to a situation in which important elements of the commons were no longer willing to remain politically inert and obedient. In other words, the ideal conceptual model of the dynastic state was losing its sway over the hearts and minds of existential men (*i.e.*, was losing legitimacy). So we see the birth and the increasing ascendency of a new conception, a new ideal: that of the people or the nation.

We have noted how most of us, projecting our own normative concepts on the past, assume that pre-revolutionary France, for example, was a French nation, its people having one language and culture distinct from those of others, sharing a national patriotism. Although it would be difficult to say when national patriotism came to predominate over local allegiances in most of France, it was certainly not before the Revolution. If one had traveled about pre-revolutionary France one would have found that the sentiment of patriotism was largely focused on villages, valleys, provinces. A man's *patrie* was his *pays*, the local scene in which he had been born and brought up. The local communities were in a large

degree self-sufficient economically and culturally. There were
Gascons from Gascony, Auvernats from Auvergne; there
were Burgundians, Picards, Lyonnais; there were Bretons,
speaking a Celtic language and giving their allegiance to
Brittany; Flemish-speaking people giving their allegiance to
Flanders; Provençals speaking a variety of Romance dialects
and giving their allegiance to Provence or Languedoc. In
the Jura and Vosges mountains the self-contained communities with their self-contained patriotisms were even
narrower. Until the French Revolution, about a third of the
French kingdom was under written Roman law, while the
rest was under customary feudal law. It was not until 1790
that internal customs barriers were abolished. There was no
uniform system of weights and measures until the metric
system was introduced in 1791.[4]

Even the word nation was slow to acquire the identity it
now has. The student-body of the University of Paris had,
in the Middle Ages, been divided into four nations: 'the
honorable nation of France,' 'the faithful nation of Picardy,'
'the venerable nation of Normandy,' and 'the constant nation
of Germany.' 'The honorable nation of France' consisted of
all those who spoke Romance languages, including what today we would call Italians and Spaniards. 'The faithful
nation of Picardy' consisted of the students from what we
now call Holland; 'the venerable nation of Normandy' of the
students from northeastern Europe; and 'the constant nation
of Germany' included the English.[5]

[4] Henri Sée, *Histoire économique de la France*, Paris, 1942, Vol. I, pp.
156-7, 223-4; Vol. II, p. 41
[5] Elie Kedourie, *Nationalism*, London, 1960, pp. 13-14. 'Il est hors de
doute,' writes M. Philippe Ariès, 'que les termes même de patrie et de nation
eurent pendant longtemps un sens très différent de celui que nous leur con-
naissons depuis le XVIIIe siècle au moins. Encore au début du XVIIe siècle
on utilisait le mot *patriote* là où nous dirions aujourd'hui *compatriote*: ils
étaient patriotes parce qu'ils étaient nés dans le même village. D'ailleurs l'ac-
ception moderne de compatriote conserve bien la même ambiguïté, quoique
nous n'y sommes plus sensibles. L'opinion commune désigna donc par patrie,

This situation began to change with the rise of dynastic states. The absolute monarchs, concerned with maintaining order within their domains and docility among the peoples under their governments, helped at some stages to promote the identification of nationality with the respective areas over which they ruled. The centralization of governmental administration in the respective capitals in which they established their courts also had this effect. To a large extent, the nation was summoned into being artificially, after the state had been created. The state preceded the nation—not, as the concept of nationalism would have it, the nation the state.[6]

We are not dealing, here, with tangibles, but rather with

---

dans la langue courante, la terre natale, le pays des ancêtres. Le mot de nation nous ramène aussi à la même conception restreinte. . . .
'La nation désignait un ensemble géographique que nous appellerions région ou province.
'Le sentiment moderne a emprunté pour se définir des termes anciens, qu'il a chargés d'un sens nouveau, ignoré jusqu'alors de l'usage commun.'
[There is no doubt that the very terms 'fatherland' and 'nation' long had quite a different sense from that which we have associated with them since at least the eighteenth century. At the beginning of the seventeenth century the word 'patriot' was still used as we would use 'compatriot': those were 'patriots' who had been born in the same village. Moreover, the modern meaning of 'compatriot' retains the same ambiguity, although we are no longer conscious of it. Common usage therefore denoted, by the word 'fatherland,' in the established parlance, one's natal land, the country of one's ancestors. The word 'nation' had the same limited meaning. . . . It denoted a geographical area that we would call a 'region' or a 'province.'
[The modern outlook has defined itself with borrowed terms from the past, giving them a sense formerly unknown in common usage.] ('Nationalisme d'hier et nationalisme d'aujourd'-hui,' *La Table Ronde*, No. 147, March 1960, p. 48.)
  [6] In Frederick the Great's *Letters on the Love of the Fatherland* (1779) he identified the fatherland with the sovereign's domain, undertaking to show the common interest of sovereign and subject in the prosperity of that domain. Cited by Kedourie, *op. cit.*, p. 11. See also pp. 77–8, where Kedourie criticizes nationalistic historiography. '. . . it is but one step,' he writes, 'from talking about the French state under Philip the Fair, Henry the Fourth, and Louis the Fourteenth, to talking about the French "nation" and its development under these monarchs. . . . France is a state not because the French constitute a nation, but rather . . . the French state is the outcome of dynastic ambitions, of circumstances, of lucky wars, of administrative and diplomatic skills.'

changing sentiments in the minds of innumerable individuals. There is nothing categorical, then, about the establishment of the French nation. It grew imperceptibly in men's minds over centuries. M. Philippe Ariès, tracing that development, cites an example of French nationalism, in the modern sense, dating from 1436, five years after Joan of Arc's execution. He also observes: 'It is probable that in the middle of the nineteenth century the national idea was still unknown to a large part of the population, especially in the rural areas. It was the school and the public school-teacher that established it definitely as a mental habit. Neither school nor teacher, however, would have been thus receptive to this sentiment without the bitterness of the defeat of 1870. Revenge is what inspired the patriotism of the teachers and their civic teaching.'[7]

*　　*　　*

Switzerland offers an even more interesting example of our habit of projecting present concepts on a past that knew them not. Historically or ethnologically, there never was such a thing as a Swiss people; and there has never been a natural geographical region corresponding to the name 'Switzerland.'[8] The Swiss people of today, and today's Switzerland, are the products of a deliberately imposed concept that responds to practical considerations rather than to any natural circumstances such as distinguish, say, the

[7] 'Il est très probable qu'au milieu du XIXe siècle, l'idèe nationale demeurait encore étrangère à une grande partie de la population, surtout dans les campagnes. C'est l'école et l'instituteur public qui la fit définitivement entrer dans les habitudes mentales. Or l'école ni l'instituteur n'auraient été ainsi sensibilisés sans l'amertume de la défaite de 1870. C'est la revanche qui a inspiré le patriotisme des instituteurs et leur enseignement civique.' *Loc. cit.*, p. 51.

[8] See Chapter I, 'The Country and its People,' of *A Short History of Switzerland* by E. Bonjour, H. S. Offler, and G. R. Potter, Oxford, 1952. Mr. Offler, the author of this chapter, is more aware than most of the element of fiction in history. Another first-rate short history of Switzerland is *Histoire de la Suisse* by William Martin, Lausanne, 1963.

Chinese from the Russians. Nevertheless, now that the Swiss nation exists, it too is projected by the romancers and the historians upon the past that never knew it.

When we read in the histories about the Roman invasions and occupations of 'Switzerland,' beginning with Julius Caesar, we should recall that nobody had ever heard of such a country in his day. When we read that 'Switzerland' was founded on August 1, 1291, we should recall that those who are said to have founded it would have been astonished to learn that they had. When we read that Jean-Jacques Rousseau was an eighteenth-century 'Swiss' philosopher, we should recall that his native city of Geneva, in which he had citizenship, was an independent city-state; that it did not join the Swiss Confederation until 1815, thirty-seven years after his death; and that there was no such thing as Swiss citizenship in the eighteenth century.[9]

August 1 is celebrated annually, with fireworks and jubilation, as the anniversary of the birth of Switzerland in 1291. What happened in 1291 was a local event that went unnoticed, at the time, in the larger world. The peasants of certain woodland valleys, lying north of the St. Gotthard Pass over the Alps, having for a generation enjoyed the independence that went with being neglected by their feudal lords, found that independence curtailed by the Holy Roman Emperor, Rudolf von Habsburg, who in violation of his promises had sent low-class ruffians as bailiffs to rule over them. (Gessler, the villain of the essentially legendary tale of William Tell, represents the type.) Fifteen days after Rudolf's death, spokesmen of the three communities that occupied the valleys met at the shore of the lake on which those valleys opened and concluded a 'perpetual' alliance to resist any attempts at like encroachment by Rudolf's

[9] Even today, primary citizenship is cantonal. The citizen of a Swiss canton is recognized *ipso facto* as a Swiss citizen, and his cantonal citizenship entitles him to a Swiss passport. In Rousseau's day, however, there was no such state as Switzerland.

successors. The remarkable thing about this alliance, as has
since transpired, is that it has so far proved to be perpetual
in fact. The association then concluded does have a continuous history and development that is represented by the
Switzerland of our day. The nation-state called 'Switzerland'
is one of its remote consequences, even though unimaginable
then.

The comparison between the association of the three
forest communities and the North Atlantic Treaty Organization in our day day springs to mind. If the defensive association to resist the common menace from Moscow should
develop, at last, into a permanent Atlantic Confederation,
men might celebrate, with fireworks and jubilation, April 4,
1949, as the anniversary of the founding of, say, 'Atlantica.'
But the signing of the North Atlantic Treaty was performed
on the world's great stage, while the conclusion of the earlier
pact, in a clearing on the lakeshore, was not noticed even by
Albert of Austria, the Hapsburg heir against whom it was
directed.

Just as Greece and Turkey later adhered to the North
Atlantic Treaty, so in the centuries that followed various
communities in the vicinity of the upper Rhine and the Alps
associated themselves with the three forest communities.
Entering into separate alliances with the original three, but
not necessarily with one another, the newcomers did not
subscribe to any comprehensive pact like the North Atlantic
Treaty. Over the generations, however, they all came to be
regarded as members of a single confederation or league.
They belonged to a sort of club of sovereign communities,
an association that was not so tight as to prevent them from
entering into alliances with one another's enemies outside the
club, or even to prevent them from waging war on one another. The name 'Switzerland' (or 'Schweiz,' from the name
of one of the original three, 'Schwyz') came to be informally
applied to their collectivity, but did not achieve official

status until Napoleon Bonaparte, in 1803, imposed the name on them along with a constitution.[10]

The sovereign confederates were first unified in 1798 by the conquering armies of revolutionary France, which forcibly created a French satellite called 'The One and Indivisible Helvetic Republic' (an example of what, in Chapter VII, I called 'the tactic of nominalism'). Before that, the cantons, as they had come to be called, had retained their sovereignties, had conducted their own foreign relations, had made war on their own, had ruled their own colonial possessions, and had maintained their own customs barriers. There had been no common coinage, no common army, no common law-courts, no common flag, no common government. Their only central organization had been a Diet at which they were represented as sovereign states by diplomatic envoys, just as the members of today's United Nations are represented in its General Assembly. The members of the Confederation made war on one another as members of the League of Nations made war on one another (*e.g.*, Italy and Ethiopia), but more readily.

In 1803, Napoleon Bonaparte, as First Consul of France, set up a Swiss Confederation, designed to be utterly dependent on him, in place of 'The One and Indivisible Helvetic Republic,' which had proved unworkable. After his fall in 1814, however, essentially the pre-Napoleonic situation was restored. The sovereign cantons regained their sovereignties, the Diet was re-established. The only important formal change was the creation of a common army (a sort of NATO army) to guard the Confederation's external frontiers. This is to say that something like the old anarchy was restored. Customs barriers rose once more between cantons. Each continued to coin its own money. The disputes that divided

[10] The name was first applied to them by their Hapsburg enemies—not entirely as a compliment, since it was a German pun of unpleasant connotations (schwyz = sweat).

Europe in the generation after 1815 also divided the cantons among themselves. It was only in 1848, after the War of the Sonderbund among them, that the present nation-state of Switzerland was founded. And even today political authority in domestic affairs is distributed among the cantonal governments to a degree that has no parallel among any of the other nation-states of the twentieth century.[11]

The Republic of Switzerland, like the German state and the Italian state, is a formal creation of the nineteenth century. The concept of a Swiss nation, on the other hand, was a gradual development, beginning in the fourteenth century and not yet completed today.[12] Although the modern Swiss state is a creation of the nineteenth century, on August 1, 1964, Switzerland celebrated her six hundred and seventy-third birthday (of which roughly the first six hundred passed unnoticed).

I have before me a short history of Switzerland by the late Professor Charles Gilliard of the University of Lausanne.[13] The first sentence tells us that Switzerland did not enter upon the stage of history until the Roman conquest: 'La Suisse n'est entrée dans l'histoire qu'avec la conquête romaine.' (By its construction, this sentence assumes a prehistoric Switzerland that, for all the reader knows, might go back to *Genesis*.) The second sentence says that Switzerland was, at the time of the Roman conquest, under the

[11] This decentralization is a luxury that Switzerland can afford by reason, *inter alia*, of its abstention from international politics. It is one of the several factors that enable Switzerland to come the closest, among all the sovereign states in the world today, to the ideal of ordered freedom. Note that there is no other country on the face of the globe in which the government would dare to issue arms and ammunition to all the able-bodied men, to be kept by them in their homes.

[12] Not completed today since most Swiss still identify themselves as much by their cantons as by the Confederation. Ask one what his country is and he will say the Valais or Berne, St. Gall or the Tessin. This situation, however, is changing rapidly as the population becomes increasingly motorized and takes to the roads; as it becomes more mobile; as its local roots are loosened.

[13] *Histoire de la Suisse*, third edition revised, Paris, 1960

occupation of some lately arrived Celtic tribes, the Helvetiae.
These tribes, not yet fixed to the soil, decided to move on
to Gaul; but Caesar stopped them and returned them to
their own country ('...les ramena dans leur pays'). It
must have been their country, one gathers, since they were
'Helvetians' and the alternative name for modern Switzerland, used by Professor Gilliard in his fourth sentence, is
'Helvetia.' Q.E.D. The history that he relates, then, is that
of this corporate person, Helvetia, beginning with her
subjugation by Rome. But this is pure fiction. The conceptual world of those days contained no such corporate person
as 'Helvetia' (or 'Switzerland') to be subjugated.

Anyone brought up on standard histories like this (which
means all of us) would find it hard to believe that Julius
Caesar, and even William Tell (if he ever existed), could never
have heard of Switzerland because there was no such thing
in their day—not as a people, not as a definable geographical
region, not as a concept. One might as well report that
Columbus invaded and subjugated the Dominican Republic.

Here, as in virtually all the histories of all our countries,
nominalism is used, retroactively, in the service of nationalism. 'Switzerland' submits to Julius Caesar in the first century B.C.; 'France' repels the Saracen invaders in 732 A.D.;
'England' is overcome by William the Conqueror in 1066;
'Mexico' is overcome by Cortés in 1519. Finding references,
in the draft of a recent doctoral dissertation, to the 'recovery'
by the Philippines of their national independence in 1946,
and to the 'recovery' of India's national independence in
1947, I persuaded the author to replace the word 'recovery'
by 'achievement.' Without my professorial authority I
doubt that I would have prevailed in this, and even so he
may have been simply humoring me. It was plain that to his
mind it only stood to reason that these countries 'recovered'
their national independence; that was the way everyone,
not only he, put it.

So the conceptual model of the nation-state, as the basic natural unit of human society, is made immortal, is projected upon a past that knew it not. Persuaded as by a tacit conspiracy that it goes back to the dawn of civilization, we can hardly fail to assume that it will continue indefinitely. This assumption, in turn, will delay its passing, just as the assumption that kings ruled by divine right delayed the passing of the dynastic state. There is bound, however, to be an increasing tension between the conceptual model and changing existential circumstances. Already in our own time we are seeing the development of this tension.

It is to our own time, then, and to the future, that we now turn.

Chapter 10

MAN'S PROGRESS

The whole succession of mankind, in the course of so many
centuries, must be considered as one selfsame man who exists
always and learns continuously.

Pascal [1]

THE basic concept, in these chapters, is of a dual world that
is evolving continuously in both its aspects, that is driven
forward by reciprocal action between the conceptual and
the existential. Concepts produce existential changes that,
in turn, require conceptual revision.[2] This irreversible secular progress has been accelerating. Until recently it was so
slow as to be imperceptible within the span of any individual's life. Only in modern times has it become so rapid, at
last, that an individual can register it vividly within the
temporal limits of his own experience. Consequently, we
have at last acquired full consciousness of our movement.
We have come to think of ourselves as being in a state of
progressive transformation; we have come to think of ourselves as being carried forward on a stream of time.

This normative concept of a world in evolution, which we
now take for granted, is itself a latter-day product of the
process of evolution. We must therefore be cautious of
projecting it upon a past that knew it, if at all, only as an
abstruse speculation of unworldly philosophers. Aristotle conceived the history of the world as the progressive imposition
of form on matter, but the world of his own experience was

[1] 'Toute la suite des hommes, pendant le cours de tant de siècles, doit être
considerée comme un même homme qui subsiste toujours et qui apprend
continuellement.' *Oeuvres Complètes*, Paris, Vol. I, p. 403

[2] A crude example: Einstein's concept of relativity led to the invention of
nuclear weapons, which have in turn contributed to making traditional concepts of national self-sufficiency obsolete.

static. The politics that he described, for example, were the politics of a static world. Change, which was in the existential world only, was accidental and chaotic rather than evolutionary. One need make even less qualification in describing the conceptual world of Dante and Thomas Aquinas; or that of the philosophers of social contract from Hobbes through Rousseau. They lived in a world that existed in consequence of special creation, a world that had been made in a week and would continue basically the same until its termination on the day of the Second Coming. Our modern sense of being carried forward on a stream of time has its first faint or occasional manifestations at the end of the seventeenth century, in the thought of the Italian, Vico, and of the German, Leibnitz (who said: 'The present is saturated with the past and pregnant with the future'). In the eighteenth century the modern theory of biological evolution begins to make its appearance in the speculations of the French naturalist, Buffon, and those of Charles Darwin's grandfather, Erasmus Darwin.

The French Revolution, in this as in other matters, is the great watershed. Those who lived through that upheaval and pondered its significance, like Edmund Burke, were impressed not only by the dramatic change that it made in a French society conceived as static, but also by the dynamics that underlay that change, by the irresistible secular forces that were bound to produce it everywhere—either by orderly evolution or, if too long resisted, by such a social explosion as had occurred in France. After the French Revolution the effort to restore the static concept of society (associated with Metternich and the architects of the Quadruple Alliance) came to seem increasingly anachronistic. From the beginning, mankind had been carried forward on the stream of time so gently that it had remained unaware of the fact; but the new rush and turbulence of the stream now made everyone conscious of riding upon it. Static philosophies would no longer do, and their place was taken by such evolutionary conceptions as those of Hegel and Marx, of Saint-Simon, of Auguste Comte, of Alexis de Tocqueville. De Tocqueville, a French aristocrat whose mind was formed by the shock of the Revolution, now presented a picture of man's political societies as evolving, over the centuries, in the direction of an ever greater egalitarianism. In his Introduction to 'Democracy in America' (1835) he wrote: 'We need a new political science for a world that is entirely new. . . . Situated in the midst of a rapid stream, we obstinately fix our eyes on some debris still visible along the shore, while the current bears us backwards towards the abyss.'[3]

Historical studies in the modern sense were a product of the same development. What we call historians from Herodotus to Gibbon were simply chroniclers and interpreters of events abstracted from universal time. But with B. G. Niebuhr and his successors in Germany, with Augustin Thierry and his successors in France, with Hallam and his successors in England, the task of history becomes that of charting the irreversible course of progress. Before ever Darwin had challenged the static concept of creation set forth in *Genesis* it has already been challenged by historical criticism in Germany.

Again, what Einstein did in the twentieth century was to replace the static three-dimensional model of the universe

[3] 'Il faut une science politique nouvelle à un monde tout nouveau. . . . Placés au milieu d'un fleuve rapide, nous fixons obstinément les yeux vers quelques débris qu'on aperçoit encore sur le rivage, tandis que le courant nous entraîne et nous pousse à reculons vers les abîmes.' (*De la Démocratie en Amérique*, Paris, 1960, Vol. I, p. 5.) De Tocqueville exemplifies a special kind of modern conservatism, first exemplified by Montesquieu and by Edmund Burke in the eighteenth century, and exemplified in the twentieth by Walter Lippmann. This conservatism is distinguished by what we call 'a sense of history,' a consciousness of the need to move with the stream of time if shipwreck is to be averted. It contrasts with the anti-historical conservatism of those whom we identify generically with the Bourbons—of a Metternich or, in our own time, a Senator Robert Taft. In the quoted statement, De Tocqueville was attacking the anti-historical conservatism.

devised by Newton in the seventeenth century with a four-dimensional model, the fourth dimension being time.

Since the French Revolution, then, we have conceived of ourselves as being carried on a flowing stream, not only in our capacity as biological organisms, but also in terms of our cultures, our civilizations, our political societies. Today we are becoming increasingly conscious of the fact that the stream is accelerating, like a river as it approaches a waterfall.

* * *

The fundamental social unit of our prehuman ancestors, one supposes, was the family group, as is the case with the hominoid apes today. The scenario which each individual found imprinted on his psyche was adapted to a natural life in the aboriginal forests. Generation after generation passed without any notable change either in the model or in the basic circumstances to which it responded. This situation, however, was not unchangeable. At some point, our pre-human ancestors became human and embarked on the unique adventure in which we are engaged today.

Perhaps this was, so to speak, part of the program of creation. Perhaps it was the inevitable consequence of an evolution driven by its own dynamics. Perhaps the slow progress of evolution had reached a point of breakthrough—like water that, for a long time rising imperceptibly in temperature, suddenly changes to steam. Perhaps catastrophic changes in the environment left the established conceptual model obsolete, confronting our ancestral hominoids with a challenge that they met by conceptual creation to replace the obsolete model.

In the earliest stages of man's development on earth he adapted himself as best he could to the aboriginal wild environment in which he found himself, hunting food that was not of his cultivation, seeking shelter that was not of his making. With time, however, he began to reform the environment, at first in quite minor ways, perhaps taking measures to protect or stimulate the wild sources of food, perhaps decorating his caves in response to obscure conceptual impulses. Agriculture and architecture developed over the millennia. Man was rising above his origins as just another wild primate to become, increasingly, a creator. He remade the face of the earth as a sculptor fashions a statue, envisaging what could be done with this swamp if it were drained by cutting a channel here, what could be done to convert this hill into a stronghold, and so forth. In our time he has, at last, physically transformed the exposed surface of the whole earth, so that, by contrast with his earliest ancestors, he lives in a man-made world, in an environment that is largely of his own creation.

In remaking his own environment man has been remaking himself. Professor Theodosius Dobzhansky cites a paper by A. Brues in which the latter suggests that

. . . a light linear body build may be favored in populations that live by hunting and pursuing game (the 'spearmen'), while a heavy muscular build is advantageous to users of blunt crushing implements and projectile weapons requiring momentary application of a large force (the 'archers'); a brawny constitution is also favored in settled agriculturists, who must be capable of sustained hard labor. Changes in implements and techniques of obtaining sustenance very likely demanded changes in the incidence of different body builds. This is perhaps one of the ways in which the evolution of culture influenced the evolution of the human physique, and vice versa.[4]

The picture we have here is of a progression driven by the dynamic interaction of the conceptual and the existential, the latter involving the human organism and its environment alike. A change in one element requires changes in other

[4] *Mankind Evolving*, New Haven, 1962, p. 231. This book gives a detailed account of modern evolutionary theory. For a brief summary of latter-day developments in evolutionary theory, relevant to the above, see my 'On Choosing our Future' in *The New Republic*, August 31, 1963.

elements that in turn require changes in the first element, so that the progression becomes automatic and self-perpetuating.

Man's developing creativity has at last become a prime factor in his own evolution, in the evolution of his earthly environment, and in the lot of other forms of life belonging to that environment. The dialectical progression had been going on at an accelerating rate. That progression is coming to a crisis in our own day. We appear to be arriving at a major turning point, like the point at which our ancestors became human and embarked on the adventure of civilization.

Pascal's concept of our successive generations as representing a single individual who continues forever to live and learn provides, if nothing else, a convenient way of thinking about the evolution of mankind. In terms of our present genetic knowledge, there is one pool of genes from which all individuals in any given line are produced, a pool that the individuals in turn transmit as a heritage to successive generations of individuals *ad infinitum*. Our bodily forms as individuals, our behavioral patterns, our consciousness, all belong to that common pool, from which we borrow our characteristics for the brief term of our individual lives. The pool might be said to represent, more than particular individuals, the fundamental existence of men—and, since its contents evolve, his progress.[5]

Just as the existential individual goes through successive stages of development—infancy, childhood, adolescence,

[5] This is not necessarily implausible. In the alternation of chicken and egg we suppose that the chicken is the end, the egg merely the means. This is because we identify ourselves with the chicken. Otherwise we might as logically suppose that the egg was the end, that the chicken represented merely the transitional step from one generation of eggs to another. We could likewise regard men as mere containers to carry over sperm cells from one generation to another. (If the free-living organisms called sperm have self-consciousness—and who can say they have not?—this would surely be their view.) Or we could say that life is represented by genes, and that individuals are simply devices for keeping them going. Who can say that what God created in his own image was not the aggregate of genes rather than the individual who transmits them? The yearling bird that flies south, unguided, over a route it

maturity—so, it appears, does Pascal's unique super-individual. This man who is the sum of all men has been manifestly growing up during the first million years of his life, and is developing with special rapidity in our present. Just as the successive stages of its future development are implicit or undeveloped in the embryo of the ordinary individual—like the cotyledons in the seed or the parts of the flower enfolded in the bud—so the stages of mankind's development represent the unfolding of what was implicit or undeveloped in its own beginnings. The evidence for this is the record of parallel developments in civilization among human societies evolving in isolation from one another. Nomadic societies in scattered parts of the world have independently entered upon the agricultural stage of civilization. In Greece, in India, and in China, peoples who were not in communication with one another simultaneously developed the same dissatisfaction with the polytheism that had, for an epoch, represented their conceptual model of creation. Simultaneously in China, in India, and in the Mediterranean, philosophy, represented respectively by Confucius, Gautama Buddha, and Socrates, became humanistic and preoccupied itself with ethical questions. The concept of plural local societies organized in local states gave way, in China and in Europe simultaneously, to the concept of one universal empire that in principle ruled the entire earth, a concept represented by the Han Empire (*c.* 200. B.C. to *c.* 200 A.D.) and the Roman Empire (*c.* 30 B.C. to *c.* 450 A.D.).[6]

---

has never before traversed, appears to share a common memory with its ancestors.

If I had to imagine the mind of God, a mind that comprehended the ultimate truth, I would imagine that it favored neither the chicken nor the egg, the individual nor the gene-pool, but saw all as parts of one whole that extends quite beyond our own vision. We are all of us like the blind men who argued about which part of the elephant was the elephant.

[6] Comparisons of this sort are potentially so illuminating that one is tempted to carry them too far. The simultaneous parallelism of Socrates, Gautama,

In the course of this broadly prescribed evolution we have at last become self-consciously aware of it; and we are becoming aware of it today as a constantly accelerating movement. Although man has been on the earth about a million years, it is only seven or eight thousand years since he began to produce civilization as we know it. Even up to some two hundred years ago this secular progress was so slow as to be inappreciable within the span of single generations. The son passed his life in essentially the same environment as his father, unaware of any permanent and irreversible progress by which mankind was advancing.[7] Evolution, natural or historical, was not a part of his conceptual store.

It was not until the end of the eighteenth century that the accelerating pace of human progress reached the point at which it began to be generally perceptible. There was the industrial revolution, itself permanent and accelerating. There was the great social transformation of which the

---

and Confucius seems to me striking. Perhaps one should add the name of Zoroaster, but we know almost nothing of him. The parallelism of the Roman and Han empires, which sometimes came into contact with each other in central Asia, is also striking. Buddhism, a universal religion of foreign origin, spread in China after the Han dynasty as Christianity, a universal religion of foreign origin, spread in the Roman Empire. One might go on to make a like comparison between Stoicism and Taoism, or between the Macedonian empire and that of the Ch'in dynasty. Since the parallels are only in the broad outline of secular developments, however, they become increasingly doubtful as one takes a more detailed view. All human societies, moreover, have not moved in line-abreast. The peoples of the New World were probably some four thousand years behind those of the Old in the development of agriculture. The Tasmanians were a paleolithic remnant in the nineteenth century, cultural contemporaries of the Crô-Magnon men who had lived some twenty thousand years earlier. Having already embarked on the scientific and industrial revolution, European civilization by the nineteenth century was well ahead of the civilization of the Orient, where the Chinese were in a state of Byzantine stagnation while the Japanese had hardly moved, as yet, beyond the feudal age.

[7] We must distinguish, here, between evolutionary changes, perceptible as such, and those chaotic, kaleidoscopic changes that have always been man's lot, that are superficial, and that, in themselves, have no perceptible evolutionary implications.

French Revolution is the classic manifestation—also perm-anent and accelerating. Today, changes that used to be imperceptible to any single generation because they took so many generations for their accomplishment take place well within the span of one individual's lifetime.

Our original disposition, as we became aware of evolution, was to make no connection between the slow evolution of species over millions of years and the evolution of human civilization in the past five to ten thousand years. Today, however, it begins to seem evident that man's history as a social and political animal is an integral part of his history as a biological organism. Just as evolution produced the human hand, so evolution is producing human civilization. The conceptual separation between nature and civilization, to which we have all been brought up, is essentially artificial. Beehives represent the natural environment of bees, whose nature it is to construct them. Our communities likewise represent our own natural environment—not completed, but as it is emerging and developing. There is a genus of tropical birds called motmots that trim their own tail-feathers to give them a racket-shape. In a narrow sense, that racket-shape is artificial, but in a broader sense it is natural, since the artifice it represents is natural to the bird.

The artifice of bees and motmots, however, has long ago become established. These are matured species, no longer evolving. Man, by contrast, is still in the process of growing to maturity. In this process he is now reaching a climax.

One speculates that not only man is involved in this pro-cess. 'Our current century,' Professor Dobzhansky writes, 'has extended evolution down to inert matter itself. Under the new dispensation not even atoms are eternal and un-changing; they, too, have histories, and their histories and those of the near and distant universes are chapters of the same grand cosmic process.'[8]

[8] *Op. cit.*, p. 4

The present crisis in man's evolution may be viewed as part of a crisis in the evolution of the universe. This view has been most completely set forth by Pierre Teilhard de Chardin in *Le Phénomène humain*.[9]

The notable thing about Teilhard's vision is that it transcends the nominal categories within which we have traditionally confined ourselves. It transcends the categorical distinctions by which we have commonly divided the world of our experience into isolated compartments unrelated to one another. It does not differentiate the astronomer's universe, which is governed by the theory of relativity, from the physicist's universe (the microcosmic universe of the atom), which is governed by quantum theory. It does not separate the inanimate world, the world of sticks and stones, from the animate world, the world of living beings. It does not make a categorical separation between biological, organic, physical life and the life of the mind, the spirit, the soul—whatever one wants to call it. Finally, it does not distinguish natural man from political man, *Homo sapiens* as a child of nature from man in civilization, as he appears to the social scientist. What his philosophy offers, in effect, is a unified-field theory, a theory that embraces all phenomena: the astronomical universe, the atomic universe, animate and inanimate being, body and mind, man and nature alike. In his vision, all being is one, and all being is moving through a single process of evolution.

Teilhard's vision of evolution begins with a uniform atomized matter thinly scattered through space. The simple atoms of this matter come together to form increasingly complex and extensive unities. Simple molecules combine in complex molecules, complex molecules in molecules of carbon, molecules of carbon in organic cells, single cells in

[9] Paris, 1955. English translation by Bernard Wall as *The Phenomenon of Man*, London, 1959. For a discussion of this book see my 'Ariadne's Thread,' in *The New Republic*, December 22, 1962.

multicellular organisms, organisms in societies (*e.g.*, termite, apian, human). Progressive combination, complexification, and unification of matter represent the direction of evolution.

The evolutionary process, of itself, produces a progressive intensification of consciousness by concentrating it. Tracing the evolution of organisms back toward their origins, one comes to a point at which life is no longer distinguishable, in which the increasingly primitive matter no longer seems to have animation. Tracing consciousness back along the line of evolution, one also reaches a point at which it is no longer perceptible. But life and consciousness, in however unimaginably reduced a form, are present in the most primitive matter, in the atom itself. As matter combines into increasingly complex and extensive unities, consciousness becomes concentrated. As it becomes concentrated, a point is reached at which it becomes perceptible, and the emergence of man finally represents the heightening of consciousness to the point where it has become self-conscious, reflecting on itself. ('Man,' Sir Julian Huxley has said, 'is nothing else than evolution become conscious of itself.')

Teilhard sees the crisis of our times as one of the great turning-points in evolution, like the point at which consciousness became self-conscious in man. 'To us in our brief span of life,' he writes, 'falls the honor and good fortune of coinciding with a critical change. . . .' It is only in our time 'that we have become conscious of the movement which is carrying us along, and we have thereby become aware of the formidable problems posed by this reflective exercise of the human effort.'[10] At this point Teilhard's vision becomes Promethean, coinciding with the Hegelian-Marxian tradition

[10] 'La chance, et l'honneur, de nos brèves existences à nous-mêmes, c'est de coïncider avec une mue . . . c'est d'avoir pris conscience du mouvement qui nous entraîne,—et par là de nous être aperçus des redoutables problèmes posés par l'exercice réfléchi de l'Effort humain.' *Le Phénomène humain*, Paris, 1955, p. 238

in which man creates himself and, in creating himself, becomes the creator of the world. The self-conscious awareness of the evolutionary process, taking the form of scientific knowledge, enables man to direct that process. Today, therefore, man is reaching the point where he will not only be able to control the mechanism of heredity, but to create new forms of life as well, by the synthesis of albuminoids. 'The dream which human research obscurely fosters is fundamentally that of mastering . . . the basic energy of which all other energies are merely servants, of taking over, all of us together, the direction of the world by grasping the very mainspring of evolution.'[11]

In Teilhard's view, then, the evolution of man and of human civilization is not to be separated from the evolution of all being. The present crisis in man's evolution is a crisis in the evolution of the cosmos itself.

No one, it seems to me, can rationally subscribe to this as a representation of ultimate truth. To be rational still means to be agnostic. As speculation, however, and as an attempt to advance human understanding, it is to be taken seriously. It liberates the mind from the absolute categories — the macrocosm and the microcosm, spirit and matter, animate and inanimate, consciousness and unconsciousness — that have traditionally confined it. It overcomes in principle the last elements of chaos by regarding all being as one: ultimately, there is only one universe for us to comprehend, not a number of different universes, each of which is to be comprehended separately from all the others.

This monism is fundamental. If one imagined the unimaginable, that physicists at last achieved total knowledge and understanding within their field, that astronomers did

---

[11] 'Le rêve dont se nourrit obscurément la Recherche humaine, c'est, au fond, de parvenir à maîtriser . . . l'Énergie de fond dont toutes les autres énergies ne sont que les servantes: saisir, réunis tous ensemble, la barre du Monde, en mettant la main sur le Ressort même de l'Évolution.' *Ibid.*, p. 278

the same for their field, social scientists for theirs, metaphysicians for theirs, and all other specialists for their respective fields, so that all knowledge was apparently achieved
—if one imagined this, but also that the knowledge and
understanding of each group of specialists had nothing to
do with the knowledge and understanding of any other,
then the human effort to achieve ultimate understanding
would remain unfulfilled. If there is an order that opposes
chaos it must be one single order that embraces all being,
for otherwise chaos remains. Part of Hegel's virtue was that
he taught us, however awkwardly, to think in these monistic
terms. This, too, is Teilhard's virtue.

I bring these considerations in, at this point, because it
seems to me that, in the back of our minds, we should always
have the liberating concept of being as an essentially indivisible whole. Our immediate concern here, however, is
with the crisis in man's accelerating evolution as a social
animal.

In the two chapters that remain I shall define the present
crisis of mankind in terms of specific developments, and
then I shall see what conclusions may be drawn for the future
of human society.

Chapter II

THE DIRECTION OF HISTORY

WE men have always been aware of the movement of time: day succeeding night and night day, the seasons following one another in their established order. What we were not aware of until recently was that this movement was going any place.

> The thing that hath been is that which shall be;
> And that which is done is that which shall be done;
> And there is no new thing under the sun.

Since the French Revolution, however, the concept of evolution has come to dominate our thinking, and to be applied at last to all being regarded as a whole. At first it was thought of as an imperceptibly slow movement, requiring centuries or millennia or more to bring about any perceptible change. It therefore seemed irrelevant to the immediate problems of living, just as the expectation that the sun will lose its heat a billion years from now is irrelevant to the immediate problems of living. Today, however, there is reason to see in evolution not only an irreversible directional movement in time but an accelerating movement as well. The image that presents itself is of a slow movement that accelerates until it is no longer a slow movement, of a movement that in its continued acceleration is approaching a dramatic culmination in our own day.

Let me cite some of the evidence for this.

The first table immediately below shows estimates of the human population of the world over the past million years, the last date being 1960. Following it are estimates of population growth in the remaining forty years of this century.[1]

---

[1] The first table is from E. S. Deevey, *Scientific American*, *203*: 195–204 (cited by Dobzhansky, *op. cit.*, p. 299), with the figure for 1960 added. The second is from Document E/CN.9/186, January 15, 1965, of the United Nations Economic & Social Council.

Estimated World Populations (Past)

Years ago	Population
1,000,000	125,000
300,000	1,000,000
25,000	3,340,000
10,000	5,320,000
6,000	86,500,000
2,000	133,000,000
310	545,000,000
210	728,000,000
160	906,000,000
60	1,610,000,000
10	2,400,000,000
0	2,990,000,000

Estimated World Populations (Future)

1980	4,269,000,000
2000	5,965,000,000

Note what kind of curve of acceleration represents these figures: a typical exponential curve of the following type:

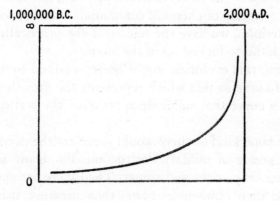

The human population increases slowly over tens of thousands of years. But the rate of increase goes steadily up, until in our time the curve that represents it suddenly approaches the vertical.

Suppose we look, now, at the development of human civilization from its beginnings. As a criterion we might take the growth of man's mastery over nature; and, to make the matter more specific, we might estimate the amount of physical power that men, at various stages, have been able to bring into their service. If one goes back to paleolithic times (say up to ten thousand years ago, when the population was still hardly more than five million), one finds that men have nothing beyond their own muscular power. With the domestication of animals they add the power of the ox and ass to their own. At some stage, in relatively recent times, they invent water-mills and windmills; they also invent sailing-ships, using the power of the wind for transport. At last, only some two hundred or two hundred and fifty years ago, they develop steam-power, using the energy locked up in coal and wood. Now begins the great industrial and technological revolution, producing spectacular increases in the efficient use of the power found in petroleum, in nitro-glycerine, in a variety of chemical compounds. Finally, within our own lifetimes, we have the release of the practically infinite power hitherto locked up in the atom.

Again, this evolution might be represented by the same kind of curve as that which represents the growth of population, a curve that suddenly approaches the vertical in our day.

The same kind of curve would represent the development of our power of military destruction. For many millennia there are only sticks and stones. Then there are spears and swords; then bows-and-arrows; then firearms, using gunpowder and constantly increasing in power. Finally, within our lifetimes, there are 90-megaton hydrogen bombs, and at last the possibility exists of constructing explosive devices of any power we wish; the possibility exists of destroying virtually all life on earth in one or two explosions.

The same kind of curve would represent the development of communications and transportation. If we take the distance a man can travel in three hours, we may estimate that for the first nine hundred and ninety thousand years, out of the last million, it would be some fifteen miles. With the domestication of the horse and the improvement of its breed it might come to be thirty miles. By the beginning of the twentieth century, with the invention of trains and automobiles, the figure goes up to about two hundred miles. Today, with manned space-vehicles, it is 54,000 miles. Again, the slowly rising curve suddenly approaches the vertical in our day.

Note that all these curves, which in one sense or another represent human power and energy, are together approaching the vertical in our day. What we see in our day, therefore, is not just a continuation of evolution, perhaps intensified. It is a culmination of some sort. It is a crisis in the evolution at least of our planet, and in the evolution of the life upon it. We are crossing a threshold. Suddenly there is a change, no longer just in degree but in kind—as when water that is rising in temperature suddenly boils. The increase in industrial and military power has, all of a sudden, become practically unlimited. The human population is, all of a sudden, filling the last habitable places on Earth. With the disappearance of frontiers, humanity is suddenly crowded in upon itself—and the social consequences are bound to be immense. A revolutionary change is already in process.

*   *   *

We should recall, at this point, that biological and cultural evolution are reciprocating parts of one process. The evolution of political societies (which concerns the modern historian) and the evolution of civilizations (which concerns the Brooks Adamses, the Spenglers, and the Toynbees) are parts of the same process as what we might call our Darwinian evolution. The development of cities and the development of nations are manifestations of man's total evolution as the development of the hive is a manifestation of the evolution of the honeybee. The ancestors of the present honeybees had a genetic constitution that was not suited to life in a hive. They were adapted to solitary or socially anarchic lives. Gradually, however, the social organization of the hive developed, and as it developed they became genetically adapted to the life of the hive. The genetic constitution of the descendants is such that they would be unable to survive in the social anarchy that was natural to their ancestors. In the cases of bee and man alike, biological and cultural evolution are one.

Now, however, man is at a crisis in his evolution. This crisis bears most immediately on his social environment, his social organization. Suddenly, because of the upswinging curves, the present social organization of mankind has become obsolete. It is in these terms that we may recognize, today, the twilight of the nation-state. The growth of industrial power, the growth of military power, the expansion of the population, the development of rapid communications —all these upswinging curves have suddenly rendered the nation-state, its geographical boundaries inherited from centuries back, unworkable.

This is a large part of the reason why we have already had two world wars (the first world wars ever) in this century. This is the reason for the great stresses and strains and crises in the international relations of our time. This provides the historical context for the problems of the 'Atlantic Community' today, for the problems of the North Atlantic Treaty Organization, for the problems of European unification and the Common Market, for the problems of African union and of Arab union, and for a host of other problems as well. In the world's great centers of political authority—whether Washington or Moscow, London, New Delhi, or Peking—the succession of crises has become constant and perpetual. Men live in a continuous state of emergency that they are coming to accept as normal. This was never known in the past, for even in exceptional periods of high emergency there was normally more time. It might, for example, take a year for one state to mount an attack on another, where today it would take a few hours. If we examine the nature of typical crises in our own time, we find them attributable to the accelerated pace of development, to those upswinging curves that are at last approaching the vertical.

We may take an instance almost at random. After the Second World War, with the whole world in revolution, the British government decided that the national security required Britain to possess its own independent nuclear panoply. It therefore set up its own manufacture of nuclear bombs and built its own fleet of 180 manned bombing airplanes (the 'V-bombers') to deliver the bombs to their targets. At the same time, it started to work on a ground-to-ground missile, the 'Blue Streak,' to replace the bombers when they became obsolete, as they would in a few years. But technology was advancing at such a pace, and the cost of weapons development was advancing at such a pace, that in June of 1960 the British government felt obliged to abandon the work on Blue Streak. It decided, then, to rely instead on an air-to-ground missile called 'Skybolt' that the American government was developing. Skybolt, fired from the V-bombers, would postpone their obsolescence. In 1962, however, the American government found that technology was advancing at such a pace, and the costs of development were multiplying at such a pace, that it felt obliged to abandon the work on Skybolt. This left the British stranded in their whole program to produce a nuclear deterrent of their own, since it left them without a replacement for means of delivery that would soon be obsolete. Immediately there was a sharp crisis, political upheavals in Westminster, and the emergency meeting between President Kennedy and Prime Minister Macmillan at Nassau, in the Bahamas, where all sorts of makeshifts were explored. What was generally evident was that Britain, by herself, simply did not have the resources to keep abreast of a progress in technology that was advancing at a constantly accelerating pace. Addressing the House of Commons on February 9, 1965, the Minister of Aviation said: 'We are at the end of the road as far as exclusive British manufacture of complicated weapons systems for an exclusive British market is concerned.'[2]

I offer one more example, this from the field of civil aviation. In the period immediately after the Second World War, competing national airlines like *Air France*, *Swissair*, and *Japan Air Lines* were developed to carry on the international air-traffic around the world in competition with one another. In late 1958, the first jet-engined airliners became available to replace the piston-engined 'planes that these airlines had been flying. Compelled by the requirements of competition to effect this replacement as quickly as possible, they substantially completed it in the next four years, but at

---

[2] In Chapter 4 of *The Arms Race*, London, 1958, Mr. Philip Noel-Baker gives figures on the growing expense of national military forces from 1884 to 1955. I cite the following random items. 'In the year before the 1914 War the six Great Powers of Europe spent £404m. on armaments; in a single year the United States alone is now spending nearly thirty-five times that amount.' Britain's defense expenditure in 1883 was £28m.; in 1955 it was £1,569m. 'British expenditure, in 1955, in terms of real resources, was nearly twice what it had been in 1939, on the eve of war.'

Since the rate of obsolescence is a function of the constantly increasing rate of development, the most advanced nations have today almost reached the point where any weapons-system is obsolete by the time it has become operational.

immense cost. Most of their old equipment, in which they had invested billions of dollars, was suddenly obsolete. Air crews and ground crews had to be completely retrained to handle the new airliners. On top of that, the increased passenger-carrying capacity of the new craft, outstripping the increased passenger-traffic, resulted in operations at a loss for most of the airlines. The total result was to place a financial burden on the national airlines that most of them were hardly able to meet. To deal with the situation, they began to enter into a variety of agreements among themselves for pooling their passenger or technical services. One example was the intergovernmental agreement by which France, Belgium, West Germany, and Italy created the 'Air Union,' representing a partial merger of their national airlines. So the crisis, too severe to be met by the individual nations alone, was met by a pooling of resources, and by moves in the direction of unification across national frontiers.

No sooner had this crisis been met, however, than the same airlines confronted the prospect of another such crisis to be produced, in the next few years, by the development of supersonic airliners. Again we see, here, the spectacle of a progress in technology that is advancing at an accelerating pace, to the point where the resources of the individual nation-state can no longer cope with it.

If all the crises of our times are not as directly attributable to the accelerated pace of change, it remains true that, typically, they occur because of it. This creates a challenge such as statesmanship has never before confronted. In the conceptual world that existed before the French Revolution statesmen were hardly under compulsion to think in terms of direction since they were not aware of movement. In the seventeenth century the Stuart rulers of England might have, as the objective of their rule, simply the perpetuation of their dynasty and their realm—of the essential *status quo*.

Today, however, statesmanship can no longer take as its objective the preservation of the *status quo*. With the world plunging forward at such a pace, the task of statesmanship is not to stop it, since that is impossible, but to steer it as best it can. Today a sense of direction is fundamental to statesmanship.

Another term for a sense of direction, in this context, is a sense of history; for a sense of history is a sense of the irreversible direction in which history is moving. When the British governments in the period after World War II recognized that colonial rule had become obsolete, that history had moved past the point at which such rule could still be imposed or maintained, then they manifested a sense of history. When the Portuguese government, a score of years after the War, fails to recognize that colonial rule has become obsolete, it shows that, like Metternich at an earlier stage, it lacks this sense. Again, when people demand the elimination of all nuclear weapons from national armaments they are also showing that they do not understand the dynamics of history, its essential irreversibility.

A basic principle of Christian conduct is to find out what the will of God is and then to put one's own will in accord with it, to will the same thing. A basic principle of statesmanship today is to determine in what direction history is moving, and then to steer the state in that direction. There are many attractive things about the world we see disappearing over the horizon behind us as we plunge forward. But it is no use trying to reverse our direction and go back. The job of statesmanship is not to return to the past, and it is not to ward off the future. It is, rather, to act as midwife for the future. The statesman must find out what the will of history is, and then will the same thing.

* * *

In what follows I take as my text the statement by Walter

Lippmann, written in 1931, that I have already cited in Chapter 1:

It is the gift of civilized man, the surest mark to distinguish him, that he can at times see through the transient and the complicated to the simple and the certain, and that he can live by that vision, and with it master or endure his lot. It is by this gift that multitudes in our Western world are today sustained through all the disorders and disappointments about them. They know that the processes of history point unmistakably to the necessity of a world-wide organization of man. They know that the inexorable pressure of the machines man has invented, of the liberties he has achieved, of the methods by which he gets his living compel him to forge unity out of the anarchy of separate states. The prophecy is as certain as it was that the American colonies had to unite, that the German principalities had to sink their differences, that the Italian communes could not forever go each its own way.

How long it will take for the prophecy to be fulfilled, no one can say. That is guesswork, and prophecy is not guessing. Prophecy is seeing the necessary amidst confusion and insignificance, and by the light which it furnishes to see more clearly how to act with purpose. The prophecy of a world moving toward political unity is the light which guides all that is best, most vigorous, most truly alive in the work of our time. It gives sense to what we are doing. Nothing else does. Without it, without the conviction that all this negotiating, and planning, and bargaining and debating is a struggle for unity and peace, it would in reality be as pointless and insane as almost daily it appears to be.

The necessary direction of history, according to Lippmann, is toward 'the world-wide organization of man,' and he lists three factors that imply as much: 'the inexorable pressure of the machines man has invented, of the liberties he has achieved, and of the methods by which he gets his living.' The pressure of these three factors 'compel him to forge unity out of the anarchy of separate states.'

Why do 'the machines man has invented . . . compel him to forge unity out of the anarchy of separate states'?

In the days before power-machinery there was no such

thing as mass-production. Cloth was woven on hand-looms in cottages to supply the needs of the family or of the immediate local community. The shoemaker made the shoes for his local community. Each local community produced its own food and its own clothing. Each was generally able to provide for itself the most efficient devices of transportation known, raising its own horses and having its own wagons built by its own wainwright. Economically as well as socially, then, the small community tended, in its self-sufficiency, to be independent of the rest of the world.

In Europe's early Middle Ages this local self-sufficiency tended to apply to military defense as well.[3] The feudal lord in his stronghold was able to provide the necessary military protection for the surrounding feudal community, which might occupy only a small valley. With the invention and development of gunpowder, however, this military self-sufficiency was lost. Cannon could knock down feudal strongholds and the walls of cities. But cannon were beyond the means of the local communities. Only the king could afford them. The king, consequently, was able to overcome the local barons and establish the much wider dynastic state that, as we saw in Chapter 9, became the matrix of the nation-state.

With the industrial revolution, with the development of power-machinery, came mass-production. One factory could produce the cloth for tens of thousands, perhaps for hundreds of thousands of people. The automobile replaced the horse, but each local community did not produce its own automobiles. Since mass-production requires mass markets, the newly industrialized nations reached out for markets beyond those of their own national populations. Since mass-produc-

[3] Local self-sufficiency in military matters had been the rule everywhere until the rise of the great empires, and even then in areas beyond their reach. With the fall of the Roman Empire it had again become the rule in Europe. It was the essence of feudalism wherever feudalism became established, whether in Europe, in Japan, or elsewhere.

tion requires vast quantities of raw materials, they began the exploitation of parts of the earth remote from their home territories. This produced the phenomenon of nineteenth-century imperialism, the contest to capture or dominate large parts of Asia, Africa, and South America. Modern machinery, then, required the unification of mankind on an ever larger scale.

Finally, the development of the machine provided the rapid communications necessary for such unification. There were the telegraph, the telephone, and radio-communication. There were fast steamships. There were railways and automobiles and trucks, with networks of highways. Finally, there were airplanes and the revolutionary pace of development in aviation.[4]

The same development continues at an accelerating pace in military technology. As the development of gunpowder made the local community indefensible in itself, so the development of nuclear weapons and inter-continental missiles (since Lippmann wrote) have already destroyed the nation-state as a self-defensible unit. And as only the king could afford cannon, so only two super-powers in our present can afford a full nuclear panoply. Economically and militarily alike, the independent nation-state has become obsolete. This bears out Lippmann's contention of a generation past that 'the machines man has invented . . . compel him to forge unity out of the anarchy of separate states.'

It is also relevant to his contention that 'the methods by which [man] gets his living compel him to forge unity out of the anarchy of separate states.' An American poultry-farmer grows chickens that are sold in the European markets. The stores of Geneva or Paris—drugstores or food-stores,

[4] In sixty years since its invention the airplane has revolutionized our conception of planetary distances. A little Genevan girl was heard to observe recently, with some awe, that New York was so far away, off on the other side of the earth, that it took seven hours to get there.

clothing-stores or bookstores—are stocked with products from half the world. The men who earn their living by making watches in the Jura Mountains would be ruined if the American market were cut off.

Finally, we may ask why, in Lippmann's words, 'the liberties [man] has achieved compel him to forge unity out of the anarchy of separate states.' The answer is that under modern circumstances political and economic freedom cannot be made secure, if they are able to exist at all, within limited areas. All the technological developments cited above extend the reach and the power of tyranny. If a single economic system, which today has to be organized on so large a scale, is under the control of one centralized authority, no local community in that area will enjoy economic freedom. In the days of radio-communication that transcends the old state-frontiers, it may be that no small community in the vicinity of a powerful dictatorship will dare to exercise full freedom of speech. Switzerland participates in the freedom enjoyed by the Atlantic community to which it belongs, but would quickly lose that freedom if the community as a whole lost it.

The initial effect of the industrial revolution, as it manifested itself in England in the early nineteenth century, may have been that of reducing economic freedom. As the industrial labor-force, in consequence of its concentration, became organized and politically powerful, however, it began to win its freedom. In the 'affluent societies' of our day, with their full employment, with the mobility of their labor-force, and with provisions for social security, we see a gain in economic freedom. In the Soviet Union, too, the transformations implicit in the production of a technologically sophisticated society are having a like effect. Political and economic freedom alike, however, can be securely maintained only on the scale of the economically independent and militarily effective unit. It was essentially this that Woodrow

Wilson meant when, confronting the threat of Kaiser William II's regime in Germany, he spoke of the need to make the world 'safe for democracy.'

Everything combines, today, to point to 'the necessity of a world-wide organization of man.' There are not only the secular developments that I have just mentioned. One may point to one simple circumstance that by itself suggests this necessity. When a nation-state, in the exercise of its sovereignty, tests a nuclear weapon within the area of its sovereign jurisdiction, it may spread radioactive poisons into the sovereign jurisdiction of half the other nation-states of the world. This in itself is an argument against what has been known, ever since Hobbes described it in his *Leviathan,* as 'the international anarchy.'

As conceptual changes result in the transformation of the existential world, so transformations of the existential world induce conceptual changes. The conceptual changes determine the direction in which statesmanship attempts to steer this hurtling world. This, and all that I have said about statesmanship in this chapter, is illustrated by my concluding quotation from Pope John XXIII's Encyclical Letter, *Peace on Earth,* issued in 1963:

Recent progress in science and technology has profoundly affected human beings and influenced men to work together and live as one family. There has been a great increase in the circulation of ideas, of persons and of goods from one country to another, so that relations have become closer between individuals, families and intermediate associations belonging to different political communities, and between the public authorities of those communities. At the same time the interdependence of national economies has grown deeper, one becoming progressively more closely related to the other, so that they become, as it were, integral parts of the one world economy. Likewise the social progress, order, security and peace of each country are necessarily connected with the social progress, order, security and peace of all other countries.

At the present day no political community is able to pursue its own interests and develop itself in isolation, because the degree of its prosperity and development is a reflection and a component part of the degree of prosperity and development of all the other political communities. . . .

As a result of the far-reaching changes which have taken place in the relations between the human family, the universal common good gives rise to problems which are complex, very grave and extremely urgent, especially as regards security and world peace. On the other hand, the public authorities of the individual political communities —placed as they are on a footing of equality one with the other— no matter how much they multiply their meetings or sharpen their wits in efforts to draw up new juridical instruments, they are no longer capable of facing the task of finding an adequate solution to the problems mentioned above. And this is not due to a lack of good-will or of a spirit of enterprise, but because of a structural defect which hinders them.

It can be said, therefore, that at this historical moment the present system of organization and the way its principle of authority operates on a world basis no longer correspond to the objective requirements of the universal common good.

Chapter 12

BEYOND THE NATION-STATE

In historical perspective, the modern nation-state will surely prove to be a passing phenomenon. I hazard the further judgment that it will be identified primarily with the nineteenth century. Historians of the future will, I think, note how rapidly it was becoming obsolete in the twentieth.

The nation-state represents the complex of ideas that we identify as nationalism. The nationalistic thinking of those who made the French Revolution, of German philosophers contemporary with them, and later of the Mazzinis, the Michelets, and the Bismarcks, was the foundation of the nineteenth-century nation-state. One would expect the nation-state itself, however, to survive for a time after nationalism had diminished, if only as the dead tree in the forest remains standing.

There is always a time-lag between a conception and its translation into forms of social organization. The new idea needs time to make its impress on the forms of a world brought up to a different idea, a different norm. The idea of nationalism developed at a time when the dynastic state still represented the norm. Generations passed before it was possible to get the dead tree of the dynastic state out of the way, replacing it with the live new nation-state. The nation-state persists through the twentieth century in like fashion. It survives even while the idea of nationalism, out of which it arose, is fading away. Today the nation-state remains standing; but nationalism—the nationalism of the nineteenth century that generated and nourished it—has been passing away. The historians of the future may plausibly be expected to note that, in the twentieth century, it was becoming obsolete as the dynastic state was becoming obsolete in the eighteenth century (although examples of the latter persisted into the twentieth).

For the moment I confine these observations to the Atlantic world, particularly to Europe. I shall come to Asia and Africa further on. In Europe the concept of the nation-state has surely been undergoing a change that diminishes its former dignity in men's minds. The same thing is happening to it as happened to the small local community when it was losing its economic and military self-sufficiency.

How is this happening?

An essential element in what impels the individual to identify himself with the sovereign state is precisely the self-sufficiency that enables it to be largely independent of the rest of the world. The individual is rescued from the sense of his own helplessness as such—his insufficiency in himself, his lack of the strength necessary for independence —by identifying himself with the majestic power of a state that can by itself defend its citizens and even, perhaps, inspire awe in their collective name. The state that can no longer do this has become inadequate to his need. He must then be attracted to what is still larger and more powerful. In the course of the evolution that I have outlined in previous chapters, the Canton of Zürich, by itself, became inadequate as a representation of power and independence for its citizens, who therefore came by a gradual and imperceptible transformation to identify themselves increasingly with the larger grouping that bears the name of Switzerland.

Taking France as a typical European nation-state, we may note how radically the whole position has changed. For centuries the problem of the defense of France was that it was too large a unit to be effectively defended from one center. Today it has become too small a unit; and while President de Gaulle, the last great representative of nineteenth-century nationalism, may insist that every great people must have the means to decide its own destiny, the fact remains that a country like France no longer has the resources that would give its people assurance of its continued ability to do so.[1] Seeing France dwarfed by the United States on one side and the Soviet Union on the other, the French people begin to think of Europe, rather than France, as the community that can stand on a level of equality in such company.

What applies to France and the French applies still more to most of the other Europeans.

The smallness of the European states in themselves is coming to be felt ever more vividly by their ordinary inhabitants, whose mobility is increasing at a revolutionary rate. On weekends and holidays, now, half the population of free Europe takes to the road—in automobiles, on motor-cycles, scooters, and motor-bicycles, or in tourist buses. In a few hours of travel they may cross two or three national frontiers, virtually without the formalities that were still required only a few years ago. All this has its generally unnoticed impact on the conceptual world in which the Europeans live, transforming it. They begin to think of themselves as inhabiting an area larger than just their own country. They begin to feel at home in a larger community. Free Europe's national frontiers, across which all this traffic flows unimpeded, come to have the aspect of internal frontiers, like those between the states in our federal union.

Add to this that Western Europe has one hydroelectric system overrunning national boundaries indiscriminately, one railway network, one international police-organization for criminal investigation, standardized road-signs and a

---

[1] 'Avoir ... pour un grand peuple la libre disposition de soi-même et de quoi lutter pour la garder, c'est une nécessité formelle.... Cela justifie simultanément l'alliance et l'indépendance.' [For a great people to have the free disposition of itself and the means with which to struggle for its maintenance is a categorical necessity.... This justifies alliance and independence simultaneously.] President de Gaulle at his press-conference of January 14, 1963.

single set of rules for road-traffic, and that tariff barriers within its confines are being reduced or eliminated. The secular trend then becomes clear. Supranational institutions, as they come into being at last, merely register overtly what has already developed imperceptibly and tacitly in men's minds.[2]

One should add to this that the experience of two devastating world wars has brought a certain discredit on the excessive nationalism that, in the eyes of most Europeans, caused them. Today the idea of conflict between European states is beginning to seem shameful to Europeans as the idea of conflict between Swiss cantons came to seem shameful to the Swiss in the course of the nineteenth century.

At this point I submit, as a general rule, that in the constant transformation of our environment we notice the appearance of the new more readily than we notice the disappearance of the old.[3] This rule has its application to the

---

[2] The reader will note that the secular trends of history are never smooth in their realization. Two forward steps are commonly followed by one backward—but the backward step is not the one that represents the trend. What we must look for is, in Walter Lippmann's words, 'the necessary amidst confusion and insignificance.'

[3] An example from the field of ornithology will serve to illustrate this rule. The species of birds to be found in any locality are constantly changing with the passage of the decades, species once common becoming scarce, species once scarce becoming common. Although the mocking-bird was virtually unknown in Washington, D.C., at the beginning of this century, it is one of the common birds of the city today. By contrast, the screech owl was a common bird throughout the eastern United States thirty years ago, but its numbers have diminished until today it is rare. If, now, one examined the ornithological literature one would find that the increase in the numbers of the mocking-bird was quite completely recorded from the outset, while the disappearance of the screech owl was not noticed until it had gone a long way toward being an accomplished fact. This is easy to understand. When the first mocking-birds established themselves in Washington, those who saw them immediately reported the fact for the records of the local Audubon Society. Thereafter, everyone was alert for mocking-birds, and as they increased from year to year made joyful records of the fact. The coming of the mocking-bird was a positive event. But the disappearance of the screech owl was a negative event. To record it would be to record the lack of something, to record something that was not. The screech owl, consequently, was not seen to disappear, and its disappearance was first noted only after it had already been accomplished in large measure.

transformations of our conceptual environment. Whatever happened to the long and bitter struggle between Christendom and Islam—the struggle marked by the Saracen advance beyond the Pyrenees, by the Crusades, by the expulsion of the Saracens from the Iberian peninsula, and by the Turkish invasions of Europe? That great ideological struggle was never won or lost, never called off, never formally concluded. There was no treaty of peace. The conflict simply faded over the years. No one noticed at any particular moment that it was now over, but a time came when it simply was no more. It went, with no one to see it going. I rather think that the same negative development is taking place in the Cold War today. Although we have not recorded the fact ourselves, history will record that after the early 1950's the Cold War was disappearing. History in these negative aspects is like the hour-hand on a clock: one never sees it move, one sees only that it has moved.

All this applies to European nationalism. Its advent is a matter of contemporary record as it was happening. There are the books by Rousseau, Fichte, Hegel, Friedrich List putting forward the nation-state as the ideal model, as nature's norm. There are the explicit and formally organized movements of national unification or national independence, led by the Mazzinis and the Kossuths. The old structure of Europe gives way before this movement. The map of Europe is remade. A new norm is established for human society, and those like ourselves who are brought up to it allow themselves to believe that it represents eternity—as the dynastic state represented eternity, as Rome represented eternity, as the Greek city-state represented it. Aristotle, as we have seen, described the Greek city-state as the eternal norm of human society at the very moment when his own pupil, Alexander, was about to gather the city-states of Greece together into his own version of the universal empire, the precursor of the Roman Empire.

Not only do we fail to notice the disappearance of the old, it is only when the old is about to disappear that we make it the subject of self-conscious study as an eternal norm of human existence. Aristotle's study of the city-state is only one of the many examples that could be cited. The institution of sea-power determined the political history of mankind for twenty-five centuries, from the days of Themistocles, but was not even given a name until Alfred Thayer Mahan published *The Influence of Sea-power on History* in 1890, just on the eve of its obsolescence under the impact of a newly developing air-power that would embrace the continents and the oceans alike. Imperialism had been the unpondered practice of the British for three centuries before it was self-consciously discovered by British statesmen like Joseph Chamberlain and by British poets like Rudyard Kipling—just at the moment when the great traditional empires, including the British, would become liabilities to be liquidated. For thousands of years men have traversed the waters in their boats under spread sails to catch the wind. It is only at the end of the nineteenth century, however, when steam-engine and gasoline-motor are replacing sail, that the art and science of sailing, including the design of sailing-craft, are developed to the utmost by self-conscious application, and that a vast literature on sailing develops. There were undoubtedly more and better studies of horsemanship produced after the advent of the automobile than before. When our universities begin studying and teaching poetry we may reasonably surmise that the great age of poetry is over. Some subconscious fear for the future of an institution that we have come to identify with our familiar world moves us to give it a name although it never had one before, to support its continued existence by making it the subject of special studies, to enshrine it in the nominal world that is so much more vivid to us than the real world. 'The owl of Athena,' said Hegel, 'takes wing only at dusk.'

Does this not apply to the history of nationalism as well? From its beginnings in the eighteenth century nationalism, although urged as a cause, was not studied as a phenomenon. Even the name 'nationalism' had not been invented. Just as the empire-builders did not know that they represented 'imperialism,' so the nation-builders did not know that they represented 'nationalism.' Scholarly self-consciousness about 'nationalism' did not manifest itself in any important way until after the First World War. When Carleton J. H. Hayes published his *Essays on Nationalism* in 1926 it seemed a novel subject.

This latter-day self-consciousness about nationalism as an institution, then, may represent the same self-consciousness that, in the case of other institutions, marked the close of the respective periods in which they flourished. It is not that the institutions do not survive in some way. City-states existed after Aristotle and Alexander the Great, and we still have San Marino with us today. The dynastic state is still represented by Ethiopia, with its dynasty claiming descent from Solomon and the Queen of Sheba. Sea-power still has a place in human affairs. Sailing ships are still in commercial use. And there are still examples of nineteenth-century imperialism, such as Angola. The self-consciousness to which I refer does not herald the complete end of the institutions themselves. It heralds merely the end of their predominance. It heralds the beginning of a new period in which they will survive as anachronisms.

*   *   *

So far I have confined these observations to the Atlantic world, particularly to Europe. The common view, however, is that they are not applicable in Asia and Africa, where nationalistic thinkings does not antedate the present century, and where it has become generally predominant only since the Second World War.

This is surely true in one important sense. The evolution of society is always at different stages in different parts of the world. Mankind does not advance in line-abreast. We may say that the Stone Ages ended five thousand years ago, but there are Stone Age societies still to be found in the Amazon Basin, in Papua, and elsewhere. The idea of nationalism first arose in Europe in the eighteenth century, but it is only now, in the second half of the twentieth, that it has at last penetrated to the far corners of the earth. If, then, instead of looking only at Europe, we look at the world as a whole, must we not conclude that nationalism, so far from ebbing, is still in its flood tide? Must we not conclude, at least, that it has begun to ebb only in one part of the world as yet?

At this point, however, we have to take account of a certain semantic confusion. 'Nationalism' is a word that does not denote a definite and immutable object. Words remain fixed while the concepts they denote undergo constant transformation. Heraclitus observed that 'there is a new sun every day'—but the word for it remains the same. 'The French Army' of Louis XIV was only nominally the same army as the one that fought the Battle of the Marne in our century. 'Turkey,' in the eleventh century, was a purely Mongol nation, a nation of people with yellow skins and slanted eyes. What is nominally the same nation today, since we use the same name for it, is a nation of white Europeans.

The name remains unchanged while the phenomenon to which it applies changes, perhaps, out of all recognition. As we saw in Chapters 4 to 8, 'Communism' as exemplified in Russia today is an altogether different ideology from what it was in 1848, when *The Communist Manifesto* was published. But the name 'Communism' has not changed in one iota, and this immutability of the name imparts an appearance of immutability to the mutable phenomenon that it denotes.

This paradox applies to nationalism as well. There is a new nationalism every day. A classic philosophical question is whether, if I replace every blade of my pocket-knife one by one over a period of time, and then replace the handle as well, it is still the same knife. The issue, here, has nothing to do with the physical reality of the knife. It is exclusively nominal, involving only the question of what we choose to call the knife: whether we choose to call it the same knife or a different knife. We have chosen to call the great anti-colonial rebellion that has swept over Asia and Africa in our day 'nationalism,' and this makes it seem absurd to say that nationalism is on the wane in the twentieth century. If, instead, we had confined the name 'nationalism' to the ideological movement that transformed Europe in the nineteenth century, calling the Asian-African movement 'anti-colonialism' or 'anti-imperialism,' then there would be no paradox in saying that nationalism is on the wane in the twentieth century.

To carry the semantic analysis a step further, there is a complex of related ideological phenomena all of which we have chosen to refer to as 'nationalism.' One of the elements in this complex is what we also call 'democracy,' the concept that sovereignty resides in the people (the 'nation') rather than in an individual ruler or an oligarchy. Another element, denoted by the French word 'étatism,' is the concept that the nation-state represents the ultimate good to which the individual should subordinate himself. Nationalism that emphasizes the state can even be anti-democratic, conceiving of the nation as a human mass under discipline from above. There are all sorts of combinations, of these two elements alone, to be found in the history of what we call 'nationalism.' The democratic element was predominant in the minds of those who originally made the French Revolution. That Revolution represented, in their minds, the deposition of the dynastic sovereign and the assumption of sovereignty by the people, the nation. With the rise of Napoleon, *étatism* became more prominent: the citizens of the nation-state must

be ready to die for it. In the German tradition from Fichte
to Hitler the individual abnegates himself completely, becoming the instrument of the state, realizing himself only
secondarily in its own realization. It was this latter kind of
nationalism that became supreme in Europe after the middle
of the nineteenth century, and that was manifested in the birth
of Bismarck's Germany. It was this kind of nationalism that
transformed Europe into a cockpit in which ruthlessly competing nation-states each tried to gain advantages for itself
at the expense of its neighbors. It was this kind of nationalism
that set off two world wars and made a shambles of Europe.
It is this kind of nationalism, I think, of which General de
Gaulle, in our time, is the last great representative.

The nationalism of Bismarck or De Gaulle, however, is
rather different from the nationalism of Nehru in India or of
Ben Bella in Algeria. It would not have been improper to
use two distinct nominal terms for these two types of nationalism, instead of using one term for both. The nationalism of
Bismarck was essentially imperialistic while the nationalism
of Nehru was anti-imperialistic. The nationalism of Bismarck was essentially anti-democratic; it viewed the world
as a cockpit in which national states competed for domin-
ance. The nationalism of Nehru simply sought liberation
from foreign domination, racial equality, and so forth.

Nineteenth-century European nationalism had, as its
objective, the supremacy of the individual nation-state.
Asian and African nationalism, in the second half of the
twentieth century, has as its objective the elimination of the
white man's supremacy and the realization of self-determination over wide and vaguely defined areas that can hardly be
said to correspond to nation-states. Bismarck was a German
nationalist, not a European nationalist; but Nkrumah is more
readily identified as an African nationalist than as a Ghanaian
nationalist. Bismarck's policy tended toward European dis-
unity, while the policy of a Nasser or a Nkrumah aims at

Arab unity or African unity. Under the rubric of 'national-ism,' then, we see in Asia and Africa the same drive toward the unification of hitherto separate communities that we see in Europe under the rubric of 'supranationalism.'

We need not, however, lose ourselves in these consider-ations. Nationalism, we may say, is ebbing in the traditional centers of the western civilization that has today become worldwide, and it does not matter in the long run whether it has, as yet, begun to ebb farther out. What counts is that the objective facts of an accelerating technological develop-ment are making the concept of the self-sufficient nation-state obsolete everywhere. What counts is such facts as that, when there is a blockage on the St. Gotthard railway-line in Switzerland, freight backs up in Scandinavia, when there is a strike at Orley Airport in Paris traffic is immediately affected at airports all around the world. These objective facts are bound to make themselves felt, at last, in men's thinking everywhere.

*   *   *

The question arises, then, of what will take the place of the nation-state.

I do not, myself, believe that any categorical answer can be made, if only because history does not proceed by abrupt steps from one category to the next. It was a gross simpli-fication to suggest, as I did some pages back, that the dyn-astic state was put aside and replaced by the nation-state. In a closer view of what happened one sees that, for the most part, the dynastic state evolved into the nation-state. When, we may ask, did the English go from the one to the other? In the period from 1804 to 1815, or from 1815 to 1830, or from 1830 to 1848, was France a dynastic state or a nation-state? What is Greece today?

Again, when did the Swiss turn away from their individual cantons to their present Confederation? The cantons persist today, and continue to have a share of their citizens' allegiance. What has happened is simply that there has been a gradual shifting of loyalty from the smaller to the larger grouping.

It is not to be expected that the European nation-states will disappear. But they already have less independence than formerly, and together they are tending to form a larger grouping that may come to enlist an increasing share of the individual's loyalties.

Is the larger grouping that we partly see and partly anticipate 'Europe,' or 'the Atlantic Community,' or 'Western Civilization,' or what Walter Lippmann has called 'a worldwide organization of man'?

These are not mutually exclusive categories. We all live within concentric circles of community. An individual may feel loyal, at one and the same time, to his village, to his province, to his nation, and to still wider communities like 'Europe' or 'Africa' or 'the Arab World' or 'Latin America.'

All we can be sure of is that, for the foreseeable future, there will continue to be a large element of anarchy in human affairs. There will be 'confusion and insignificance.' The element of accident will continue to appear dominant in any close-up view. The management of chaos will continue to be the preoccupation of practical statesmanship. But all the time, barring total disaster, we shall be moving toward a permanent, worldwide organization of man.

We may confidently believe, as well, that we shall be moving toward some ultimate order beyond our present imagining.

POSTSCRIPT

In the main text I deliberately refrained from descending into the philosophical depths that I had already explored in *Men & Nations*. The main text simply suggests, without argument or elaboration, that the evolution of human society is part of a process by which an initial chaos is made into a final order. No one will question that the creation of order out of chaos is, at least, the direction of human effort. Some will say that this is all there is to it, that we men are free to make whatever order we please out of the chaos that surrounds us, that the very notion of order is our own invention, that there has never been any order in the universe aside from what we have chosen to project upon it.

Like every ontology or theology, this necessarily begs the question of beginnings. The man who says that Jehovah created the world cannot say how Jehovah came to be in the first place. The man who says that order is a property of the human mind only cannot say how that property came to belong to it. The predominant philosophical thinking of our day holds that such questions should not even be asked, since, being unanswerable, attempts to answer them can lead only to pernicious mystifications. I agree that they are unanswerable at the present stage of our development, but I think we should not pretend that they do not exist. The awareness of their existence in itself imposes a certain humbleness that seems to me salutary (although there are those who dislike them precisely on this account). It seems to me not altogether good that we men should glorify man to the extent of regarding him as the sole creator. He has indeed created his environment in large measure, transforming the earth, but he did not create the raw material of that environment. Whatever he has wrought with the atom, for example, the atom itself is not of his creation.

In the same way, I find it too limiting to attribute all order in the universe, the concept of order itself, to man alone. This is to commit oneself to a sort of collective solipsism—and solipsism makes no more sense than anything else.

If we drop solipsism, then we can hardly deny the existence in the universe of an order independent of man. There are, for example, natural laws of mass and inertia that account for the revolution of our planet and the course it takes about the sun. At the present stage of our knowledge we men may have formulated these laws erroneously or inadequately, but the regularity of the Earth's movement, and of other phenomena, hardly allows us to doubt that they exist, and that they exist in exemplification of a natural order antedating man's arrival on the scene.

Although using the fanciful language of the sixteenth century, Richard Hooker was stating a truism when he wrote:

Now if Nature should intermit her course, and leave altogether, though it were but for a while, the observation of her own laws; if those principal and mother elements of the world, whereof all things in this lower world are made, should lose the qualities which now they have; if the frame of that heavenly arch erected over our heads should loosen and dissolve itself; if celestial spheres should forget their wonted motions, and by irregular volubility turn themselves any way as it might happen; if the prince of the lights of Heaven, which now as a giant doth run his unwearied course, should as it were through a languishing faintness begin to stand and to rest himself; if the moon should wander from her beaten way, the times and seasons of the year blend themselves by disordered and confused mixture, the winds breathe out their last gasp, the clouds yield no rain, the earth be defeated of heavenly influence, the fruits of the earth pine away as children at the withered breasts of their mother no longer able to yield them relief; what would become of man himself, whom these things now do all serve? See we not plainly, that obedience of creatures unto the law of nature is the stay of the whole world?[1]

Those of us who deny that there is any natural order might find ourselves discomfited if, suddenly, it ceased to operate.

[1] *Laws of Ecclesiastical Polity*, I, iii, 3

I suppose, then, that there was an order in the universe before man developed. The order which man tries to realize, to bring out of chaos, is a pre-existing order. If this is so, then human creation must, in its essence, be discovery.

There are some things that one can say about this partially apprehended pre-existing order. It is susceptible of expression in logical terms. In other words, it matches the order in our own minds that we call logic. It is, in fact, co-extensive with that order, and therefore it is a logical order. Under the circumstances, the term 'Logos,' applied to it in the opening sentence of the Fourth Gospel, has seemed to me appropriate as well as convenient.

The reader must not think that I am propounding, here, some abstruse, elaborate, and perhaps mystical doctrine. What I have in mind is a rationalism that, far from needing volumes of argument, is so simple that in these first few paragraphs of my postscript I have said it all. I do not see how any physical scientist could question it, since his professional concern is, precisely, to discover the pre-existing natural order that it postulates.

The position of social scientists tends to be different because the element of chaos is so prominent in the material with which they deal. The astronomer's world is governed by laws that all the stars and their satellites obey; there are no exceptions to its regularity. This is as true of the physicist's world. The social scientist, however, is likely to find that each society is in large measure unique, and that its behavior changes from generation to generation if not from year to year. We explain this by saying that the world of human society is artificial, by contrast with the natural world that obeys natural law; that social organization represents human artifice, and is therefore subject to human tinkering at will. The attempts that are made to find significant regularities that apply absolutely to all mankind are generally fruitless. It follows that social scientists are less disposed than physical scientists to believe in a pre-existing natural order. Dealing more with the characteristics of particular societies than with the nature of society generically conceived, they are less disposed to attach the value of reality to anything that is not an empirically determined datum. They, more than the physical scientists, tend to the view that questions directed at what lies beyond the empirically knowable are better left unasked.

We ought, I think, to be asking ourselves what we mean by artificial, and what relation it has to natural. We could call the beehive an artifice of the bees, but since we know that it is the nature of bees to construct hives we regard it as natural. Is it not the nature of man to construct societies?

We might answer that it is not the nature of man to construct any one particular kind of society. The various particular societies he constructs are the products of a self-consciousness unknown to the bees. They are the products of self-conscious activity, and self-conscious activity is what we mean by artifice.

One may carry the argument deeper, then, saying that self-conscious activity must represent the nature of man.

What is notable about this self-conscious activity, however, is that it is so chaotic, so apparently free of any natural order. Man's artifice is free to produce developments in a multitude of directions, without the hindrance of any narrow limits set by a natural order. Experiencing this, philosophers are prone to conclude, as does the present French school of Existentialists, that there is no natural order to which man is subject, but that he makes his own order as he pleases. This kind of thinking is especially characteristic of urban intellectuals, those who, inhabiting the great cities of the world, live entirely in environments provided by human artifice and know little at first hand of a natural world beyond them.

Man and his artificial worlds, however, exist in a sea of nature, and if one assumes that the cosmos represents a

single order one must believe that man's artificial worlds
are ultimately a part of nature. This could be a play on
words, since we are implicitly defining 'nature,' here, as the
whole of being. It is more than a play on words, however,
for what I am saying is that the order in our human minds,
which has such various expressions in our artifice, is not
unrelated to the pre-existing natural order in the universe.
Ultimately, the logical order that we see expressed in the
physical universe is the same as the logical order native to
our minds. What we are trying to express in our artifice is a
natural order that we are able to comprehend, as yet, only
imperfectly. It is a man-made order proximately, but not
ultimately. Ultimately, it is what I have called the Logos.

* * *

I have connected the physical sciences with the Logos in
the above paragraphs, and I have indicated that I think the
Logos is not irrelevant to the social sciences. The concept of
the Logos seems to me also to illuminate and be illuminated
by the arts—or, more simply, by art. Here is where I almost
despair of making myself clear to the many persons in whose
lives literature, music, and the graphic arts play hardly any
part.

It is not irrelevant to what I have said here that an appreciation of music is common among physicists, rare among
men in politics and social scientists. Music is the most
abstract of the arts and, accordingly, the one that approaches
most nearly the purity of an ineffable perfection for which
the human mind gropes. Abstract painters have tried to
achieve something like this in their painting, but painting where it is most effective in suggesting perfection still
has a representational element in it with which music can
more readily dispense. The language of literature, also, is
explicit and denotive as the language of music is not.

Music, in respect of an abstract conceptual perfection,

is not unlike mathematics, and has been associated with it at least since the days of Pythagoras. One might say that two and two make four in mathematics and music, while in the other arts it has to be two apples or two of something else concrete. The other arts can hardly dispense with an existential adulterant; and though much modern painting undertakes to dispense with it one cannot yet say that it has achieved the heights of greatness in doing so.

Physicists tend to live in the same world of perfection as mathematicians and musicians. They live in a world of abstract natural laws that contains (essentially as abstractions) electrons, protons, and neutrons in various established relations with one another. This is to say that they live close to the Logos. In their professional preoccupations they transcend the accidental and chaotic. They are perfectionists, perfectionism being an addiction to the Logos. This explains why physicists are so much more likely than social scientists to have a taste for music.

By contrast, men who are temperamentally suited to politics cannot be perfectionists; for politics, as we noted in the first three chapters, is the management of chaos by makeshift, it is mediation between the existential and the conceptual worlds, it is compromise. To revert momentarily to the theme of the first chapter, anyone who was a perfectionist would be a misfit in a foreign office.

Perfectionists may be drawn to mathematics and physics, but they are unlikely to be drawn to politics, to political science, or to any of the social sciences. Conversely, those who are drawn to the social sciences are unlikely to be perfectionists. Therefore they are unlikely to be attracted by music or the other arts, and the concept of the Logos itself is unlikely to appeal to them.

The Logos is the subject of the arts as it is of astronomy and physics. My own view is that, in a large sense, it is the concern of political studies as well. Political philosophy is therefore handicapped where those who represent it are insensitive to what the arts represent. They are likely, then, to be insensitive to the natural order without which there is no meaning, without which there is only chaos. They are likely to be uncomprehending, like humorless persons reacting to a humorous remark. Without the sense of what is represented by the arts, without an artistic sense, there is no human creativity. Without it, consequently, there can be no creative achievement in the field of politics or in that of political studies.

There cannot be an order for one category of being and not for another. I repeat here, by way of conclusion, what I said in Chapter 10. If one imagined the unimaginable, that physicists at last achieved total knowledge and understanding within their field, that astronomers did the same for their field, social scientists for theirs, metaphysicians for theirs, and all other specialists for their respective fields, so that all knowledge was apparently achieved—if one imagined this, but also that the knowledge and understanding of each group of specialists had nothing to do with the knowledge and understanding of any other, then the human effort to achieve ultimate understanding would remain unfulfilled. If there is an order that opposes chaos it must be one single order that embraces all being, for otherwise chaos remains.

Ultimate truth, if ever we achieve it, will surely turn out to be artistic truth.

INDEX

THIS is not a reference book and cannot be made to serve as such. Persons and events are mentioned, not for the purpose of conveying information about them, but to illustrate ulterior points. The following partial index has been supplied, nevertheless, in the thought that the reader who wishes to return to any passage already read may find that it offers him a short-cut.

For the principal subjects treated and the themes developed the reader will find it more useful to consult the elaborated table of contents that begins on page 7.

INDEX

INDEX

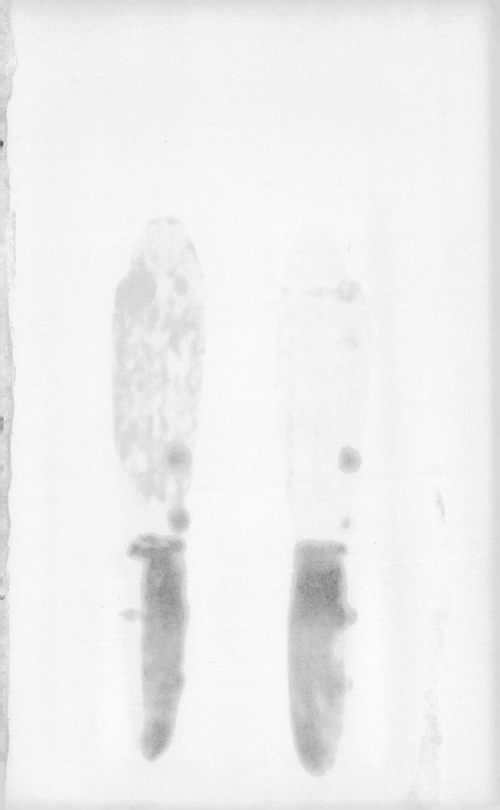

8/1/66

DATE DUE

GAYLORD   PRINTED IN U.S.A.